VEGAN

SNACKS & MUNCHIES

VEGAN

SNACKS & MUNCHIES

PLANT-BASED NIBBLES, SNACKS, DIPS & SWEET BITES

RYLAND PETERS & SMALL
LONDON • NEW YORK

Senior Designer Sonya Nathoo
Designer Emily Breen
Commissioning Editor Alice Sambrook
Production Controller David Hearn
Editorial Director Julia Charles
Art Director Leslie Harrington
Publisher Cindy Richards
Indexer Vanessa Bird

First published in 2018
by Ryland Peters & Small
20–21 Jockey's Fields
London WC1R 4BW and
341 E 116th Street, New York, 10029
www.rylandpeters.com

10 9 8 7 6 5 4 3 2

Recipe collection compiled
by Alice Sambrook

Text copyright © Amy Ruth Finegold, Anya
Ladra, Caroline Artiss, Chloe Coker, Dan
May, Dunja Gulin, Hannah Miles, Jenna Zoe,
Jordan Bourke, Laura Washburn, Vicky Jones
and Ursula Ferrigno.

Design and photographs copyright ©
Ryland Peters & Small 2018

ISBN: 978-1-78879-032-1

A CIP record for this book is available from
the British Library.
US Library of Congress CIP data has been
applied for.

Printed in China

Notes
• Both British (Metric) and American
(Imperial and US cups) measurements are
included in these recipes for your
convenience, however it is important to
work with one set of measurements and not
alternate between the two.
• Buy unwaxed citrus fruit and wash before
zesting. If you can only find treated fruit,
scrub well before using.
• Always check the product packaging to
ensure the particular brand of ingredient
you are buying is vegan.

CONTENTS

INTRODUCTION

Snacks and munchies are the mood-boosting, energy-bolstering treats that everyone looks forward to. What's an enjoyable weekend without a bowl or platter of indulgent munchies to share? Or a good gym session without a nutritious snack to re-fuel afterwards? They really are essential pick-me-ups at any time of day, from a few bites with mid-morning coffee to an afternoon morsel when energy is flagging. Evidence has shown that munching between meals is a healthy habit, but only, of course, when the food is unprocessed and full of good, nourishing ingredients. With this book of over 65 recipes, you can quit processed convenience snacks full of salt, sugar and dairy and choose a healthier way to graze that looks out for your well-being and the well-being of the planet, too. Once you have your favourite recipes down, try making big batches at the start of the week, ready to grab and go when hunger strikes.

Sample savoury recipes from Nuts, Veggies & Other Nibbles such as the ridiculously moreish Bombay Mix or spicy Masala Popcorn. Creative vegetable-based morsels like Spicy Tomato Kale Chips and Sesame-crusted Green Beans use plenty of herbs and spices to bring out the delicious flavours of the natural produce. Energy Bites, Balls & Bars features convenient recipes perfect for an active lifestyle. Try packing super-healthy Pure Energy Bars or Berry & Baobab Bites in your bag before a hike. Or whip up a batch of Chocolate & Avocado balls, they taste like truffles but are full of healthy fats and nutrients! In the Dips & Dippers chapter, you can find deliciously satisfying plant-based dips such as Hot Spinach & Artichoke Dip or summery Zesty Almond Pesto and Lighter Guacamole. Get busy with the selection of easy recipes for dippers, from seeded crackers to breadsticks and tortilla chips. Look no further than the Party Pieces section for a varied array of snacks and munchies for entertaining at casual gatherings. Courgette/zucchini & Walnut Canapés are ideal for when you want something a bit smart with minimum effort or whip up a batch of Jalapeño Onion Rings for a crowd-pleasing nibble. Finally, Sweet Treats is a sweet-toothed vegan's dream come true – from Coffee Toffee Cookies to Bean & Cashew Brownies, these delightful bites are as guilt-free as they come.

Whatever your reasons for avoiding animal products, whether ethical, environmental, health-benefits or a mixture of all three, you'll find a whole host of recipes here that will revolutionise your snacking and munching. Satisfy bad cravings with this virtuous food, which proves once and for all that plant-based snacking can be every bit as delicious as it is good for you!

NUTS, VEGGIES & OTHER NIBBLES

MASALA POPCORN WITH FRESH LEMONADE

TOGETHER, THIS SPICY HOME-POPPED CORN AND REFRESHING LEMON SODA ARE THE IDEAL COMBINATION OF SWEET, SALTY AND SPICY – AND THE PERFECT PROVISIONS FOR A NIGHT IN WATCHING MOVIES.

1 tablespoon popcorn kernels

½ teaspoon sea salt

1 tablespoon chaat masala (to make your own, mix a pinch each of garam masala, ground cumin, ground fennel seeds, ground ginger, black pepper and paprika)

LEMONADE

500 ml/2 cups naturally sparkling water

freshly squeezed juice of ½ lemon

1 teaspoon xylitol or stevia

ice, to serve

SERVES 1

For the masala popcorn put the popcorn kernels in a non-stick saucepan over a medium heat and place the lid on top. As soon as you hear the corn start to pop, turn the heat down to low. Remove when all corn has popped – about 45–60 seconds. Toss the freshly popped corn with the salt and chaat masala and place in a big bowl. You have full permission to eat the entire serving yourself!

For the fizzy lemonade put some ice in a large glass and pour in the sparkling water and lemon juice. Add the sweetener and stir well.

Variations

Basil and oregano: add 1 teaspoon olive oil to the popcorn kernels in the pan. Pop as above, then remove from the heat and toss in 1 tablespoon each of dried basil and dried oregano.

Cheesy truffle: add 1 teaspoon truffle-infused olive oil to the corn kernels in the pan. Pop as above, then remove from the heat and toss in 3 teaspoons nutritional yeast, which will give the popcorn a slightly cheesy flavour.

Sweet treat: add 1 teaspoon coconut oil mixed with 1 teaspoon vanilla extract to the corn kernels in the pan. Pop as above, then remove from the heat and toss in a generous pinch of ground cinnamon.

THAI GREEN CURRY POPCORN

FULL OF THE ENTICING FLAVOURS OF THAI CUISINE, THIS
POPCORN IS ONE SATISFYING SNACK. YOU CAN BUY SEVERAL
EXCELLENT VEGAN VARIETIES OF THAI GREEN CURRY PASTE
IN SUPERMARKETS AND IT CERTAINLY SAVES A LOT OF TIME,
HOWEVER, YOU CAN ALWAYS MAKE YOUR OWN FROM SCRATCH.
YOU MAY NEED TO ADJUST THE QUANTITY USED IN THE POPCORN
TO TASTE ACCORDING TO THE STRENGTH OF YOUR PASTE.

100 g/6 tablespoons extra virgin coconut oil, plus 1–2 tablespoons for cooking the popcorn

90 g/⅓ cup popcorn kernels

1 tablespoon vegan Thai green curry paste

1 teaspoon lemongrass purée*

grated zest of 1 lime

2 teaspoons sugar

1 generous tablespoon freshly chopped coriander/cilantro

sea salt and freshly ground black pepper

SERVES 6

Heat 1–2 tablespoons of coconut oil in a large lidded saucepan with a few popcorn kernels in the pan with the lid on. When you hear the kernels pop, carefully tip in the rest of the kernels and replace the lid. Shake the pan over the heat until the popping stops. Take care when lifting the lid as any unpopped kernels may pop from the heat of the pan. Tip the popcorn into a bowl, removing any unpopped kernels as you go.

Melt the remaining extra virgin coconut oil in a small saucepan set over a low heat. Add the curry paste, lemongrass purée and lime zest and cook for a few minutes, stirring all the time.

Pour the Thai-flavoured coconut oil over the warm popcorn, sprinkle with the sugar, coriander/cilantro, salt and pepper, and stir well so that the popcorn is evenly coated. This popcorn can be eaten warm or cold.

*Lemongrass purée is available in most supermarkets, but if you are unable to find it you can substitute a 2-cm/1-inch piece of lemongrass, finely chopped and pounded in a mortar and pestle with 1 tablespoon of vegetable oil.

BOMBAY MIX

WHO CAN RESIST A GOOD, SALTY BAR SNACK? THE INGREDIENTS LIST IN THIS RECIPE IS FAIRLY LONG, BUT THE WHOLE THING TAKES ABOUT 10 MINUTES TO PREPARE. FEEL FREE TO OMIT ANY INGREDIENTS YOU DON'T HAVE TO HAND.

3–4 tablespoons peanut oil (or almond oil, coconut oil or grapeseed oil if you don't have peanut oil)

70 g/½ cup yellow split peas

35 g/¼ cup cashews

35 g/¼ cup peanuts

35 g/¼ cup pumpkin seeds

110 g/2 cups plain corn flakes (with no added sugar)

3 tablespoons unsweetened flaked coconut

3–4 slices dried mango, finely chopped

2 tablespoons raisins

½ teaspoon ground cumin

¼ teaspoon paprika

1 teaspoon ground turmeric

½ teaspoon sea salt

½ teaspoon onion powder

2 teaspoons vegan Worcestershire sauce

freshly squeezed juice of 1 lime

1 green chilli/chile, deseeded and sliced

Heat the oil in a saucepan over a medium heat. Fry the split peas, cashews, peanuts and pumpkin seeds for a few minutes until the split peas have softened and are cooked through. Add the corn flakes and toss until crispy.

Add all the remaining ingredients. If the mixture gets dry, feel free to drizzle in 1 tablespoon of water. Stir to combine, remove from the heat and discard any remaining moisture or oil.

Allow to cool, then refrigerate in an airtight container until you're ready to serve it. It will keep for up to 1 week. If it softens after a few days, toast it slightly in the oven.

SERVES 8

SALTY TRAIL MIX

THIS TRAIL MIX IS A VERY SATISFYING BLEND OF NUTS, SEEDS AND SUCCULENT FRUITS – GREAT FOR SNACKING.

100 g/²⁄₃ cup sunflower seeds

100 g/²⁄₃ cup pecans

100 g/²⁄₃ cup almonds

50 g/¹⁄₃ cup pumpkin seeds

3 tablespoons goji berries

3 tablespoons raisins

2–3 tablespoons pure maple syrup

1 teaspoon salt, or to taste

non-stick dehydrator sheet

dehydrator

Soak the almonds and pecans in separate bowls of cold water for 4 hours; and the sunflower seeds and pumpkin seeds in separate bowls of cold water for 30 minutes.

Drain the nuts and seeds and toss with the remaining ingredients in a bowl.

Spread the mix out on the dehydrator sheet. Dehydrate at 46°C/115°F for 20–24 hours, flipping the mix over halfway through. It is ready when the nuts and seeds are crunchy. Store in an airtight container until needed.

SPICY ALMONDS

SLIGHTLY SWEET WITH A TOUCH OF CHILLI/CHILI AND CUMIN, THESE IRRESISTIBLE ALMONDS ARE A PERFECT AFTERNOON SNACK!

150 g/1 cup almonds

1 tablespoon pure maple syrup

2–2¹⁄₂ teaspoons chilli/chili powder

1¹⁄₂ teaspoons minced or finely grated onion

³⁄₄ teaspoon ground cumin

¹⁄₂ teaspoon salt

non-stick dehydrator sheet

dehydrator

Soak the almonds in a bowl of cold water for 6 hours.

Thoroughly drain the almonds, then toss them with all the remaining ingredients in a bowl to coat evenly.

Spread the almonds out on the dehydrator sheet. Dehydrate at 46°C/115°F for 24 hours, flipping them over halfway through. The almonds are ready when they are crunchy. Store them in an airtight container until needed.

SERVES 2–4

TARALLI

THESE LITTLE OLIVE OIL AND BLACK PEPPER SNACKS HAIL FROM PUGLIA AND ARE VERY ADDICTIVE. IN ITALY, THESE ARE SERVED BEFORE A MEAL WITH APERITIVOS, BUT REALLY THEY MAKE EXCELLENT SNACKS AT ANY TIME OF DAY. YOU COULD TRY ADDING CRUSHED FENNEL SEEDS AS THEY WORK VERY WELL TOO.

150 g /1 cup plus 3 tablespoons Italian '00' flour, plus extra for sprinkling and kneading

40 g/⅓ cup semolina (fine)

1 teaspoon freshly ground black pepper or 2 teaspoons lightly crushed fennel seeds (optional)

2 teaspoons sea salt

70 ml/⅓ cup dry white wine

70 ml/⅓ cup extra virgin olive oil

2 baking sheets, oiled

MAKES 30

Mix together the flour, semolina, pepper or fennel seeds, half the salt, wine and oil. Knead on a floured surface until smooth and elastic, about 2 minutes. Place the dough in a lightly oiled bowl, cover and leave to relax for approximately 45 minutes to 1 hour.

Bring 900 ml/scant 4 cups water to the boil and add the remaining salt.

Halve the dough and cut each half into 10 pieces. Keep the remaining dough covered with a damp kitchen cloth while you work. Roll one piece of dough into a 50-cm/10-inch long rope. Cut the rope into 5 pieces, then roll each piece into 10 cm/4 inch ropes. Connect the ends to form an overlapping ring. Continue with the remaining dough, keeping the taralli covered.

Preheat the oven to 180°C (350°F) Gas 5.

Boil the rings in batches until they float, approximately 3 minutes. Transfer with a slotted spoon to the prepared baking sheets and bake in the preheated oven for about 30 minutes until golden. Cool on wire racks and enjoy.

SPICY TOMATO KALE CHIPS

KALE CHIPS ARE A GREAT ALTERNATIVE TO PROCESSED CRUNCHY
SNACK FOODS BECAUSE KALE IS ONE OF THE BEST THINGS YOU CAN
PUT IN YOUR BODY. TURNING THE LEAVES INTO CRUNCHY CHIPS
IS A BRILLIANT WAY TO SNEAK MORE VEGGIE GOODNESS INTO
YOUR DIET IN A FUN WAY. THESE ARE MOREISH BUT BEAUTIFULLY
LIGHT TOO, SO EATING TOO MANY IN ONE GO IS NOT A PROBLEM!

**1 head of curly kale or 1 packet
of pre-chopped curly kale (about
50 g/1¾ oz.)**

1 large tomato, quartered

**3 sun-dried tomatoes (dry not marinated
ones, with no added sugar)**

½ teaspoon paprika

¼ teaspoon ground cumin

pinch of sea salt

⅛ –¼ teaspoon cayenne pepper

freshly ground black pepper

baking sheet lined with foil

Preheat the oven to 200°C (400°F) Gas 6.

Tear small pieces of kale off the stems and place them
in a colander. Wash them, then dry them as thoroughly as
possible – ideally they should be completely dry. Place the
dry pieces in a large bowl.

Put the tomato quarters and sun-dried tomatoes in
a food processor. Pulse until smooth, scraping down the
sides of the bowl as you go. It won't seem like a lot of
mixture, but the idea is just to flavour the kale rather than
cover it in a thick sauce. Add the paprika, cumin and salt,
then as much cayenne and black pepper as you like,
depending on how spicy you want your chips to turn out.
Process the mixture again, then pour it into the bowl of
kale. Using your hands, toss the kale so that it is evenly
coated in the spicy tomato mixture.

Spread the kale pieces onto the prepared baking sheet
and bake in the preheated oven with the door slightly ajar
for about 14–16 minutes. You will know the kale is ready
when it is totally crispy and thin. If you can resist eating it
all immediately, store it in an airtight container for about
4–5 days at room temperature.

NYC-STYLE GLAZED NUTS

STALLS SELLING FRESHLY ROASTED, SWEET GLAZED NUTS CAN BE
FOUND ON MANY STREET CORNERS IN NEW YORK CITY. WITH THIS
RECIPE, YOU CAN RECREATE THE DELICIOUS TREAT IN A HEALTHIER
WAY. THIS VERSION IS PRETTY AUTHENTIC, USING GROUND
ALMONDS/ALMOND MEAL IN PLACE OF WHITE SUGAR TO GIVE
THEM THAT CLASSIC SLIGHTLY GRITTY TEXTURE.

2 tablespoons coconut oil

2 tablespoons agave syrup

1 teaspoon grated nutmeg

**350 g/about 2½ cups mixed nuts, eg.
almonds, peanuts, cashews, hazelnuts,
soy nuts**

**2 tablespoons xylitol or stevia, or other
granulated sweetener**

**½ teaspoon arrowroot or cornflour/
cornstarch**

50 g/½ cup ground almonds/almond meal

baking sheet, lined with foil

SERVES 6

Preheat the oven to 200°C (400°F) Gas 6.

Put the coconut oil in a medium saucepan and heat
until melted. Remove from the heat and allow it to cool for
a few minutes, then stir in the agave syrup and nutmeg.

Add the nuts to the saucepan and toss to coat well in the
liquid. Using a slotted spoon, transfer the nuts to a bowl.
Reserve the remaining liquid in the pan for later.

Put the sweetener and arrowroot or cornflour/cornstarch
in a high-speed blender and blitz until finely ground.
Combine this with the ground almonds/almond meal, then
tip into the bowl of nuts. Mix well, to coat, then transfer the
nuts to the prepared baking sheet. Pour the reserved liquid
over the nuts and toss them.

Roast the nuts in the preheated oven for 30 minutes, then
allow to cool for 5 minutes before serving. Store in an
airtight container for up to 5 days.

CHILLI RELLENOS

CHILLI RELLENOS IS ONE OF MEXICO'S MOST ICONIC DISHES. THIS VEGAN VERSION IS A LIBERAL TAKE ON THE ORIGINAL, WHICH OFTEN COMES STUFFED WITH MEATS OR CHEESES, BUT IT RETAINS THE HEAT AND FLAVOURS THAT THE DISH IS KNOWN FOR.

½ red onion, finely diced

1 tablespoon olive oil, plus extra for brushing

1 medium tomato, chopped

65 g/1 cup brown mushrooms, chopped

150 g/¾ cup ready-made tomato pasta sauce

1 tablespoon tomato purée/paste

1 tablespoon balsamic vinegar

1 teaspoon vegan Worcestershire sauce

½ teaspoon chilli/chili powder

generous dash of hot (pepper) sauce, to taste

30 g/⅓ cup walnuts, plus extra chopped, to serve

3 pointed red peppers, halved and deseeded

freshly ground black pepper

baking sheet, greased and lined with foil

Preheat the oven to 200°C (400°F) Gas 6.

Put the red onion and olive oil in a frying pan/skillet set over a medium heat. Fry until browned, then add the chopped tomato and mushrooms, tomato sauce, tomato purée/paste, balsamic vinegar, Worcestershire sauce, chilli/chili powder and hot (pepper) sauce. Season with black pepper, then simmer for a few minutes, allowing the mixture to reduce slightly.

Remove from the heat and transfer to a food processor with the walnuts and pulse lightly – you want the mixture to be a little chunky.

Lightly brush the outsides of the pepper halves with olive oil and place them skin-side down on the prepared baking sheet. Spoon the tomato mixture into the pepper halves and bake in the preheated oven for 35 minutes until brown.

Remove the peppers from the oven and garnish with chopped walnuts before serving.

SERVES 2-3

SESAME-CRUSTED GREEN BEANS

THESE MAKE REALLY ELEGANT NIBBLES, AND ARE GREAT AS
A PRECURSOR TO AN ASIAN MEAL. THEY ARE CRUNCHY AND
DELICIOUS AS WELL AS BEING PACKED FULL OF NUTRIENTS.

1 tablespoon ground flaxseeds/linseeds

3 tablespoons tamari soy sauce

1 tablespoon agave syrup

60 g/½ cup sesame seeds

1 packet of fresh green beans (about 24),
trimmed*

*baking sheet lined with baking parchment
or foil*

Preheat the oven to 180°C (350°F) Gas 4.

Put the flaxseeds/linseeds, soy sauce and agave syrup in a
wide bowl and whisk with a fork until mixture has thickened
slightly. Put the sesame seeds in another wide bowl.

Place each green bean into the marinade, one at a time,
then dip into the sesame seeds. Once fully coated, place
on the prepared baking sheet.

Bake the beans in the preheated oven for 12 minutes –
they should be softened on the outside but still crunchy
on the inside.

*If you're serving these beans as finger food, you may want
to cut them in half to make them easier to eat in one bite.
Otherwise, leave them whole.

SERVES 4-6

CHICKPEA FRITTERS

KNOWN IN SICILY AS PANELLE, THESE SOFT-YET-CRUNCHY
FRITTERS ARE MADE BY BOILING CHICKPEA/GRAM FLOUR, LETTING
IT COOL, THEN CUTTING INTO SQUARES AND FRYING.

250 g/2 cups chickpea/gram flour, sifted

1 teaspoon salt

1 tablespoon freshly chopped flat-leaf parsley

3 tablespoons olive oil

coarse sea salt and freshly ground black pepper

SERVES 4-6

Whisk the chickpea/gram flour into 1 litre/4¼ cups of water until there are no lumps, then season with the salt.

Heat the batter gently in a saucepan, stirring constantly, until it boils and thickens. Simmer the mixture for about 15 minutes, whisking constantly. Stir in the parsley and cook for another 5 minutes.

Pour onto the prepared baking sheet and smooth out the surface. The mixture should be no more than 1 cm/⅜ inches thick. Leave to cool for several hours to allow the mixture to solidify.

Preheat the oven to 200°C (400°F) Gas 6.

Cut the set batter into triangles, squares or, to make chunky chips, batons about the size of your largest finger.

When the oven is hot, put the olive oil on a clean baking sheet and heat in the oven for a few minutes, then using a spatula, transfer the fritters to the hot oil, flipping over once to coat both sides with oil. Put in the preheated oven for about 20 minutes, until the fritters are crisp on the surface and starting to brown, then turn over and cook for another 10 minutes. Sprinkle with coarse sea salt and black pepper and serve immediately.

MARINATED OLIVES & PADRÓN PEPPERS

THESE OLIVES ARE MADE IN ADVANCE BUT THE PADRÓN PEPPERS NEED TO BE COOKED AND THEN SERVED STRAIGHT AWAY. MILD GREEN CHILLIES/CHILES CAN BE SUBSTITUTED IF YOU CAN'T FIND PADRÓN PEPPERS.

QUICK MARINATED OLIVES

200 ml/¾ cup good olive oil

3 garlic cloves, bruised and skin on

large sprig of fresh rosemary

1 hot red chilli/chile, very thinly sliced

grated zest of 1 lemon

400-g/14-oz. can black pitted olives

PADRÓN PEPPERS

20 pimientos de Padrón (small green fresh Spanish peppers)

1 tablespoon good olive oil

sea salt flakes

SERVES 4-6

To make the quick marinated olives, put the oil, garlic and rosemary in a saucepan and heat very gently, until the first few bubbles begin to rise up to the surface. Remove the pan from the heat, add the chilli/chile and lemon zest and set aside to cool.

Meanwhile, drain, rinse and pat the olives dry on paper towels. Place them in a large jar or bowl. Once the infused olive oil has cooled, pour it over the drained olives. Leave at room temperature for a minimum of 2 hours before serving, periodically stirring or shaking (if they are in a jar!) to allow the flavours to infuse the olives. The longer you can leave them the better the end results will be.

To make the simple Padrón peppers, wash and pat the peppers dry on paper towels but do not destalk them. Heat the oil in a frying pan/skillet over a medium heat and fry the peppers in small batches, turning frequently, until they begin to change colour and the skin starts to puff up. Remove from the pan and drain on paper towels. Season with salt flakes and serve.

Tip: Be warned! Although Padrón peppers are generally very mild, about 1 in 10 can have a real hot kick. You can dress the peppers with a little of the oil from the marinated olives, which is delicious!

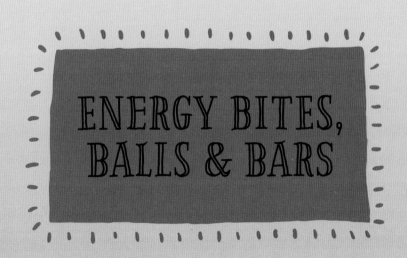

ENERGY BITES,
BALLS & BARS

CHOCOLATE & AVOCADO BALLS

IT'S HARD TO TELL THESE CREAMY, DECADENT BALLS OF GOODNESS ARE TOTALLY VEGAN! THE AVOCADO IS FULL OF NUTRIENTS TO KEEP YOU GLOWING FROM THE INSIDE OUT.

280 g/10 oz. vegan dark/bittersweet chocolate (70 per cent cocoa solids)

1 ripe avocado

pinch of sea salt

½ teaspoon vanilla extract

1 tablespoon agave syrup or caster/granulated sugar

COATINGS (CHOOSE ONE OF THE BELOW OR A MIXTURE OF ALL)

desiccated/shredded coconut

chopped pistachios

chopped flaked/slivered almonds

chopped hazelnuts

cocoa powder

MAKES 20

Break the chocolate into small pieces and pop into a heatproof bowl. Set the bowl over a pan of barely simmering water and stir to melt. Once melted, stir in the agave syrup or sugar. Set aside to cool slightly.

Scoop the avocado flesh into a large mixing bowl, discarding the stone. Add the salt and mash it to a very fine pulp.

Add the avocado to the cooled melted chocolate with the vanilla and gently fold together. Pop the mixture in the fridge to set for 30 minutes, or until much more firm. Meanwhile, put the coatings in shallow bowls.

Next, roll the chocolate mixture into balls. Scoop a small tablespoon into the palms of your hands and quickly roll it into a ball, then immediately roll in whichever coating you want. Continue until you have used up all the chocolate mixture. Put the balls in an airtight container and chill for at least 30 minutes before serving. Store in the fridge and eat within 2 days.

BERRY & BAOBAB BITES

GOJI BERRIES HAVE BEEN USED IN CHINESE MEDICINE FOR
THOUSANDS OF YEARS. THEY ARE PARTICULARLY GOOD FOR YOUR
SKIN, AND, ALONG WITH THE BLUEBERRIES AND BAOBAB, THEY
CONTAIN HIGH LEVELS OF ANTIOXIDANTS AND VITAMIN C. AFTER
MAKING THESE LITTLE BITES OF HEAVEN, YOU'LL FEEL LIKE
YOU'VE ALSO HAD A MOISTURISING HAND TREATMENT, TOO!

130 g/1 cup almonds or cashews

pinch of sea salt

50 g/½ cup goji berries

85 g/½ cup dried wild blueberries

4 dates, pitted

1 tablespoon baobab fruit powder

1 tablespoon virgin coconut oil

20 g/¼ cup desiccated/shredded coconut

SERVES 4

Put the nuts and salt into a food processor. Blitz until they are chunky but not finely ground, then add the berries, dates, baobab fruit powder and coconut oil, and blitz until the mixture starts clumping together – it doesn't have to be puréed or too finely ground, you still want bits.

Roll the mixture into balls with your hands – your hands will feel very soft after making these with the coconut oil in them! Roll each ball in the coconut to coat and enjoy.

Store these balls in an airtight container in the fridge for 3–4 weeks. They can also be frozen for up to 3 months, simply defrost before serving.

COCONUT & SPIRULINA BALLS

SPIRULINA IS AN AMAZING SUPERFOOD AND A VERY POWERFUL
ALKALIZER – SOME SAY THAT ALKALIZING FOODS HELP BRING THE
BODY TO ITS 'HAPPY PLACE' WHERE IT CAN FUNCTION AT ITS VERY
BEST. THESE GLORIOUSLY GOOD-FOR-YOU ENERGY BALLS ARE AN
EASY AND DELICIOUS WAY TO GET YOUR DAILY SUPERFOOD DOSE.

90 g/½ cup dates, pitted

65 g/½ cup cashews

1 large teaspoon coconut oil

1½–2 teaspoons spirulina powder

1 large teaspoon matcha powder (green
tea powder)

about 20 g/¼ cup unsweetened
desiccated coconut

MAKES 16

Soak the dates in a bowl of water for 30 minutes, but
no longer than that.

Put the cashews in a food processor and pulse for about
30–45 seconds until a thick meal has formed.

Rinse the dates, wipe off any extra moisture and add them
to the food processor along with the coconut oil, spirulina
and matcha powder. Process until a large ball starts to
form. Remove the blade and take the processor bowl off
the stand.

Using damp hands to prevent the mixture from sticking too
much, pinch off pieces of the mixture about the size of
whole walnuts. Roll them into balls between the palms of
your hands.

Roll each ball in the desiccated coconut to coat it evenly,
then place on a plate or board. Repeat with the rest of the
mixture.

Refrigerate the energy bites for at least 20 minutes. Store
in the fridge in an airtight container for up to 3 weeks.

TAHINI PROTEIN BITES

A LOT OF ENERGY-BITE SNACKS USE EITHER OATS OR DRIED FRUIT
AS A BASE, BUT WHAT IF YOU WANT TO AVOID BOTH? IF YOU'RE
SIMPLY LOOKING FOR A QUICK WAY TO EAT A GOOD PROTEIN
AND FAT COMBO, POWER UP WITH THESE BITES. DON'T LET THEIR
CUTENESS FOOL YOU – THEY TASTE LIKE DESSERT BUT WILL
KEEP YOU TRIM.

2 scoops vegan protein powder

3 tablespoons coconut flour

¾ tablespoon granulated stevia

3 tablespoons coconut oil

2 tablespoons tahini

½ teaspoon pure vanilla extract

**12-hole heart-shaped chocolate
mould or silicone ice tray (optional)**

MAKES 12

Put the protein powder, coconut flour and stevia in a large
mixing bowl and stir to combine.

If your coconut oil is solid, gently melt it in a saucepan
or pot set over a medium heat until liquefied.

Pour the melted coconut oil, tahini and vanilla into the dry
mixture and stir well.

Scoop the batter into the mould or roll into small balls.
Cover and put in the fridge to chill for at least 20 minutes,
or until firm.

Turn out the bites from the mould and enjoy.

CAROB & COCOA 'FUDGE' BARS

THESE MAGIC BARS HAVE THE CREAMINESS AND DENSITY OF
FUDGE AND THE NUTS PROVIDE A WONDERFUL CRUNCH. CAROB
AND COCOA BOTH HAVE DISTINCTIVE TASTES THAT COMPLEMENT
ONE OTHER; TO MAKE THIS 'FUDGE' MORE INTERESTING, IT IS
COMPRISED OF TWO SEPARATE COCOA AND CAROB LAYERS.

225 g/1½ cups cashew nuts

100 g/⅔ cup dates, pitted

80 g/⅔ cup dark raisins

½ teaspoon ground cinnamon

pinch of salt

3 tablespoons raw cocoa powder

3 tablespoons carob powder

60 g/½ cup Brazil nuts, cut into slivers

20-cm/8-inch baking dish, lined with
clingfilm/plastic wrap

Put the cashew nuts, dates and raisins in separate bowls,
cover with warm water and allow to soak for 1 hour.

Drain the soaked nuts and fruits and put in a food
processor with 4–5 tablespoons water, cinnamon and salt.
Blitz until smooth.

Divide the mixture in half. Add the cocoa to one half and
the carob to the other. Mix well.

Spoon the cocoa mixture into the lined baking dish and
spread level. Now spoon the carob mixture into the dish on
top of the cocoa and spread level. Scatter Brazil nuts
evenly over the top, pressing them gently into the fudge.
Cover and freeze for at least 2 hours.

You can also refrigerate the fudge but it will remain slightly
sticky. It's much easier to slice it when it's frozen, and it
tastes a lot better – even better than chocolate ice cream!

MAKES ABOUT 16

HAND-ROLLED MACAROONS

THESE GORGEOUS COCONUTTY BALLS ARE THE PERFECT MID-MORNING MUNCHY AS WELL AS A GREAT ENDING TO A MEAL WHEN YOU JUST WANT A FEW BITES OF SOMETHING SWEET.

COCOA COCONUT

40 g/½ cup desiccated/ shredded coconut

30 g/¼ cup cocoa powder, plus extra for rolling

3 tablespoons agave syrup

3 tablespoons coconut oil

1½ teaspoons pure vanilla extract

WINTER SPICE

40 g/½ cup desiccated/ shredded coconut, plus extra for rolling

30 g/¼ cup ground almonds/almond meal

4 tablespoons sugar-free blackstrap molasses

1 teaspoon granulated stevia

½ teaspoon grated fresh or ground ginger

½ teaspoon ground cinnamon

¼ teaspoon ground nutmeg

3 tablespoons coconut oil

APPLE AND CINNAMON

40 g/½ cup desiccated/ shredded coconut, plus extra for rolling

30 g/¼ cup ground almonds/almond meal

4 tablespoons sugar-free apple purée (or applesauce)

¾ teaspoon ground cinnamon

1 teaspoon granulated stevia

1 teaspoon pure vanilla extract

3 tablespoons coconut oil

Each of these macaroons can be made in the same way. Put all of the ingredients into a mixing bowl and stir to combine.

Shape the mixture into balls using your hands or a melon baller, arrange on a clean baking sheet and transfer to the fridge to chill for at least 20 minutes, or until firm.

Meanwhile, sift a little extra cocoa powder or coconut, depending on which macaroons you are making, onto a wide plate.

Remove the macaroons from the fridge and roll them in the cocoa powder or coconut before serving.

SERVES 6

PURE ENERGY BARS

KEEPING A STASH OF THESE BARS IN YOUR FRIDGE, EACH NEATLY
WRAPPED UP AND READY TO GO, WILL LEAVE YOU FEELING READY
FOR ANYTHING. THEY ARE EQUALLY AMAZING FOR BREAKFAST OR
AS A PICK-ME-UP SNACK. YOU CAN USE MILLET FLAKES TO MAKE
THESE BARS GLUTEN-FREE AND INSTEAD OF APRICOTS ANY OTHER
DRIED FRUITS. ALSO, TRY ADDING ORANGE JUICE AND ZEST
INSTEAD OF LEMON FOR THE POPULAR COCOA-ORANGE COMBO.

2 very ripe bananas

3 tablespoons extra virgin coconut oil

zest of 1 organic lemon plus 1 tablespoon lemon juice

15 dried apricots, diced

1 teaspoon rum (optional)

200 g/2¼ cups fine rolled oats

¼ teaspoon ground cinnamon

⅛ teaspoon bourbon vanilla powder

3 tablespoons raw cocoa powder

pinch of sea salt

18 x 18-cm/7 x 7-inch shallow dish or baking pan

MAKES 8

Peel the bananas and put them in a deep plate before mashing them thoroughly with a fork. If the coconut oil has solidified, set the jar in a bowl of boiling water until the oil begins to liquify. Add the oil, lemon zest and juice, apricots and rum, if using, to the mashed bananas and stir well.

In a large bowl, combine the rolled oats, cinnamon, vanilla, cocoa and salt. Mix and add the banana mash to the dry ingredients. Use a spatula to combine the ingredients really well – there should be no dry patches of oats and the dough should be thick and sticky.

Now take the dish or small baking pan and cover its bottom and sides with clingfilm/plastic wrap. Place the dough in it and use a spatula or your hands to press down the mixture until you get an even layer about 1.5 cm/½ inch thick. Wrap well with more clingfilm/plastic wrap and refrigerate for at least 2 hours (but best if left overnight).

Unwrap the clingfilm/plastic wrap and cut into 8 even bars; wrap each one separately and use up during the week!

BROWNIE BARS

NEED A HEALTHY WAY TO SATISFY CHOCOLATE CRAVINGS? TAKE
THESE FIVE INGREDIENTS AND BLITZ YOURSELF A RAW, VEGAN
CHOCOLATE BROWNIE IN NO TIME AT ALL!

300 g/2 cups cashews

120 g/¾ cup walnuts

110 g/1 cup raw cacao powder

100 g/⅔ cup soft dates, pitted

1 tablespoon coconut oil

agave or pure maple syrup, to taste
(optional)

deep, 22 x 15-cm/9 x 6-inch baking pan or
container, lined with baking parchment
(optional)

Put all the ingredients in a food processor and blitz until
they are well combined and you have a smooth and rather
sticky paste. If it is too dry, add 2 or more tablespoons of
agave or maple syrup.

Scrape the mixture into the prepared baking pan and
smooth level with your hands. If you don't have the correct
size of pan, lay a sheet of clingfilm/plastic wrap on a board,
scrape the mixture onto the sheet and shape it with your
hands into a rough rectangle about 2.5 cm/1 inch thick.
Wrap in clingfilm/plastic wrap.

Refrigerate for 1 hour before cutting into 6 squares
to serve.

MAKES 6

VERY CHERRY BALLS

SWEET, PRETTY, EASY TO PACK AND NUTRITIOUS, THESE LITTLE
BALLS ARE ESSENTIALLY JUST FRUIT AND NUTS TURNED INTO
SMALL TREATS AND ROLLED IN A TASTY COATING. THEY MAKE
YOU FEEL LIKE YOU'RE EATING SOMETHING SPECIAL!

4–6 dates, pitted

50 g/⅓ cup dried cherries

225 g/¾ cup ground hazelnuts

1 tablespoon ground flaxseeds

ground cinnamon, to taste

Bourbon vanilla powder, to taste

a little raw almond milk, if needed

**coconut flour, cocoa powder or coarsely
ground nuts, for coating**

MAKES 15–20

Put the dates and cherries in a bowl, cover with warm water
and allow to soak for 20 minutes or until soft.

Drain the dates and cherries and reserve the soaking water.

Put the soaked dates and cherries in a food processor and
blitz until blended into a thick paste, adding a little of the
reserved soaking water, if needed.

Mix together the ground nuts and seeds and add cinnamon
and vanilla powder to taste. Add the puréed fruit and mix
well to get a smooth, thick paste. Add little milk if the
mixture is too dry.

Take portions of the mixture about the size of chocolate
truffles and roll into balls with your hands. Roll them in any
(or all) of the suggested coatings.

Refrigerate for at least 1 hour before serving.

SPORTS BITES

THESE LIGHT BITES PACKED FULL OF ENERGY-BOOSTING
INGREDIENTS ARE THE PERFECT FUEL FOR PHYSICAL ACTIVITIES
WHERE YOU NEED A SMALL, COMPACT SOURCE OF ENERGY THAT
YOU CAN EASILY STOP TO EAT AT REGULAR INTERVALS, FOR
INSTANCE THEY WOULD BE PARTICULARLY GOOD TO BRING
ON A HIKE. THE NATURAL FRUIT SUGARS PROVIDE ENERGY AND
THE ALMONDS PROVIDE PROTEIN, COCONUT OIL AND HEMP SEEDS
BRING THE HEALTHY FATS, AND THE COCONUT OIL HELPS
REGULATE METABOLISM. ALL THIS AND THEY TASTE AMAZING TOO!

**50 g/½ cup raw almonds (use raw ones if
you can, to make this an all-raw recipe)**

60 g/½ cup dried apricots

2 tablespoons shelled hemp seeds

1½ tablespoons coconut oil

vanilla extract

Put the almonds in a food processor and pulse until
crumbly. Add the apricots and process until well
incorporated and the mixture starts to come together into
a paste. Add the hemp seeds and coconut oil, plus vanilla
extract to taste.

Divide the mixture into 8 and roll each portion into a ball
between the palms of your hands.

Freeze the sports bites for at least 15 minutes. Store in the
fridge in an airtight container for up to 3 weeks.

DIPS & DIPPERS

AVOCADO MISO DIP WITH ROOT VEGETABLE CHIPS & DUKKAH

THIS GUACAMOLE WITH A JAPANESE TWIST IS SO QUICK AND EASY
TO MAKE AND THE DUKKAH, AN EGYPTIAN NUT AND SPICE MIX,
ADDS A DELICIOUS THIRD TEXTURE TO THIS SNACK ATTACK.

20 g/2½ tablespoons blanched almonds

20 g/2½ tablespoons blanched hazelnuts

2 tablespoon sesame seeds

1 tablespoon cumin seeds

1 tablespoon coriander seeds

1 tablespoon dried mint

120 g/4 oz. avocado

1 tablespoon brown vegan rice miso paste

1 tablespoon freshly squeezed lemon juice

2 teaspoons tahini

2 teaspoons extra virgin olive oil

1 small garlic clove, crushed

ROOT VEGETABLE CHIPS

2 medium beetroot/beets

2 medium parsnips

olive oil

sea salt

mandoline grater

2 baking sheets, lined with baking
parchment

Preheat the oven to 200°C (400°F) Gas 6.

Peel, top and tail the beetroot/beets and parsnips, then
using a mandoline, cut into thin slices. Pat dry with paper
towels. Place in a bowl and toss lightly with olive oil to give
them a very thin coating. Toss with a little sea salt then lay
out, not overlapping, on the two prepared baking sheets.
Roast in the preheated oven for 5–8 minutes, keeping an
eye on them as they burn easily. Remove and leave to cool.

Reduce the oven temperature to 180°C (350°F) Gas 4.

Roast the almonds for about 8 minutes and the hazelnuts
for about 5 minutes on separate trays and Leave to cool.

Meanwhile, in a dry frying pan/skillet over a medium heat,
fry the sesame, cumin and coriander seeds for 1–2 minutes
until fragrant. In a food processor, blitz the spices, roasted
nuts, seeds, dried mint and ¼ teaspoon of sea salt until
finely ground, no longer though, as the nuts will begin to
release oils. Spoon the mixture into a bowl and set aside.

Blitz the avocado in the food processor with the miso
paste, lemon juice, tahini, olive oil and garlic until smooth.
Taste and adjust the seasoning if necessary.

Serve the vegetable chips with the avocado miso dip with
some of the dukkah sprinkled over. To eat, dunk the chips
into the dip and then back into the remaining dukkah,
which will cling on to the wet dip.

SWEET POTATO HUMMUS WITH BREADSTICKS

SWEET POTATO IS A DELICIOUS ADDITION TO THE CHICKPEAS IN THIS HUMMUS AND CRUNCHY BREADSTICKS COMBO.

1 sweet potato, unpeeled

3 garlic cloves, unpeeled

½ x 400-g/14-oz. can of chickpeas

1 fresh red chilli/chile, finely chopped

handful of fresh coriander/cilantro leaves, chopped

2 tablespoons olive oil

grated zest and freshly squeezed juice of ½ lime

BREADSTICKS

300 g/2¼ cups plain/all-purpose flour

2 teaspoons fast-action yeast

2 teaspoons salt

1 teaspoon sugar

120–150 ml/½–⅔ cup lukewarm water

4 tablespoons/¼ cup olive oil

pinch of mixed dried herbs

pinch of cayenne pepper

salt and freshly ground black pepper

SERVES 4-6

For the sweet potato hummus, preheat the oven to 180°C (350°F) Gas 4. Roast the sweet potato in a baking pan for 30–40 minutes until very soft. Add the garlic cloves to the pan about 20 minutes before the end of the cooking time. Remove from the oven and, when cool enough to handle, peel the potato and garlic, discarding the skins.

Put the sweet potato, garlic, chickpeas, chilli/chile, coriander/cilantro, oil and lime zest in a food processor and blitz until smooth. Season with salt and pepper to taste.

For the breadsticks, preheat the oven to 170°C (340°F) Gas 4. Combine the flour, yeast, salt and sugar in a bowl. Make a well in the centre, then pour in the oil and water. Stir until combined and a soft but not sticky dough comes together. Knead the dough for about 10 minutes. Cover with oiled clingfilm/plastic wrap and leave it to rise in a warm place for 40–60 minutes or until doubled in size.

Divide the dough in half and roll half the dough out into a flat rectangle about 0.5–1 cm/¼–⅜-inch thick, then cut it into 1-cm/⅜-inch-wide strips. Roll the strips into pencil-width tubes. Repeat with the other half of the dough. Spread the dried herbs, cayenne pepper, salt and pepper on a board, then roll the breadsticks in them and put them on a floured baking sheet. Bake in the preheated oven for 20–30 minutes until golden. Cool on a wire rack before serving with the hummus.

BEETROOT DIP WITH SEEDED AMARANTH CRACKERS

YOU EAT WITH YOUR EYES WITH THIS DIP! BEETROOT/BEET IS AS NUTRITIOUS AS IT IS COLOURFUL.

2 garlic bulbs, unpeeled

4 beetroot/beets, tops and bottoms trimmed

3 tablespoons flaxseed oil

1½ teaspoons ground sumac

1 teaspoon cumin seeds

freshly squeezed juice of 1 lemon

1 teaspoon sea salt and freshly ground black pepper, to taste

fresh coriander/cilantro, to garnish

SEEDED AMARANTH CRACKERS

45 g/⅓ cup amaranth flour

40 g/⅓ cup milled flaxseeds

40 g/¼ cup sunflower seeds

1 teaspoon sea salt

¼ teaspoon onion powder

20 g/⅛ cup pumpkin seeds

2 tablespoons milled hemp seeds

1 tablespoon melted coconut oil, plus extra for greasing

2 baking sheets, lined with foil

For the dip, preheat the oven to 180°C (350°F) Gas 4.

Wrap the garlic in foil and put on one of the prepared baking sheets. Wrap the beetroot/beets in a separate sheet of foil and put on the same baking sheet. Roast the beetroot/beets and garlic for 30 minutes, then remove the garlic and set aside. Roast the beetroot/beets for a further 30 minutes or until tender, then allow to cool.

Peel the garlic and the beetroot/beets (this is the messy part so feel free to wear gloves!) and blend them in a food processor with the flaxseed oil, sumac, cumin seeds, lemon juice, salt and pepper. Add more flaxseed oil as required to reach the desired consistency.

For the crackers, preheat the oven to 150°C (300°F) Gas 2. Grease the second prepared baking sheet with coconut oil.

Pulse all of the dry ingredients in a food processor – you can leave the seeds in a roughly chopped state, if you prefer more texture. Then add the coconut oil and 60 ml/¼ cup water and blend again until all the ingredients come together into a dough. Roll the dough thinly onto the prepared baking sheet and bake in the preheated oven for 45–50 minutes. Set aside to cool, then break into pieces. Store in an airtight container until ready to serve.

Transfer the dip to a serving bowl, garnish with fresh coriander/cilantro and serve with the crackers.

WHITE BEAN & SPINACH DIP WITH WHOLEGRAIN CROSTINI

USING SEED OILS IN DIPS IS AN IDEAL WAY TO LOAD UP ON
OMEGA 3S. THIS BEAUTIFUL GREEN SUMMERY DIP LOOKS
GREAT GARNISHED WITH FRESH HERBS AND TASTES AMAZING
SMOTHERED ON CRUNCHY CROSTINI, AS HERE.

410 g/2½ cups white beans

freshly squeezed juice of 1 lemon

freshly squeezed juice of 1 clementine

1 garlic clove, peeled

50 g/1 cup spinach

3 tablespoons flaxseed oil

sea salt and freshly ground black pepper,
to taste

CROSTINI

1 wholegrain baguette or
6 wholegrain rolls

120 ml/½ cup garlic-infused olive oil

For the crostini, preheat the oven to 180°C (350°F) Gas 4.

Slice the baguette or rolls into 1-cm/½-inch slices. Brush both sides of the sliced baguette or rolls with garlic-infused olive oil then arrange the pieces on a baking sheet. Season with salt and pepper.

Bake the slices in the preheated oven for 20 minutes, turning once so both sides cook evenly and brown. Transfer the crostini to a wire rack to cool then serve with the white bean dip.

For the dip, blend all of the ingredients together in a food processor and serve. It's as easy as that! If you like, you can add the spinach at the end and leave it coarsely chopped so the little dark green flecks are visible.

SERVES 4

AUBERGINE DIP WITH ALMOND CHIA CRACKERS

BABA GANOUSH IS A STAPLE OF LEVANTINE CUISINE. THIS TASTY DIP IS SOMETIMES MADE WITH TAHINI PASTE, SO FEEL FREE TO ADD A SPOOONFUL FOR EXTRA RICHNESS IF YOU LIKE. YOU'LL FIND THE ALMOND CHIA CRACKERS ARE THE PERFECT SCOOPING TOOLS.

800 g/2 large aubergines/eggplants

2 tablespoons grapeseed oil

½ teaspoon Himalayan salt

2 garlic cloves

2 tablespoons freshly squeezed lemon juice

3 tablespoons flaxseed oil

sea salt and freshly ground black pepper, to taste

ALMOND CHIA CRACKERS

60 g/½ cup almond flour

30 g/¼ cup coconut flour

30 g/¼ cup ground chia seeds

¾ teaspoon sea salt

½ teaspoon onion powder or 1 chopped small onion

60 ml/¼ cup olive oil

Preheat the oven to 200°C (400°F) Gas 6.

Cut the aubergine/eggplant in half and pierce the skin and flesh several times. Put on a baking sheet, drizzle with the grapeseed oil, sprinkle with the salt and bake in the preheated oven skin-side up for 35–40 minutes or until the flesh is tender. Remove from the oven and cool in a bowl of iced water. This will make it easier to peel away the skins.

Peel and discard the skins and add the flesh to the garlic, lemon juice and flaxseed oil in a food processor. Blend, season with salt and pepper and store in the refrigerator until you are ready to serve.

For the crackers, preheat the oven to 180°C (350°F) Gas 4.

Add all of the dry ingredients to a mixing bowl. Then add the oil and 60 ml/¼ cup water and mix to form a ball with your hands. Chill in the refrigerator in clingfilm/plastic wrap for 20 minutes, then roll out as thinly as possible on a rectangular non-stick baking sheet. Bake in the preheated oven for 15 minutes, then leave to cool and cut into pieces.

Transfer the dip to a serving bowl and serve with the almond chia crackers.

HOT SPINACH & ARTICHOKE DIP

THIS HEALTHY DIP IS ONE OF THOSE THINGS THAT WHEN YOU
START EATING, YOU JUST CAN'T STOP. BUT REALLY, THERE'S NO
REASON TO STOP – IT'S ALL GOOD STUFF – SO ENJOY!

1 x 390-g/14-oz. can artichokes

30 g/¾ cup macadamia nuts

200 ml/¾ cup almond milk (or non-dairy milk of your choice)

½ tablespoon salt

2 garlic cloves

3 tablespoons nutritional yeast

½ white onion, diced

olive oil, for sautéing

½ tablespoon arrowroot starch

400 g/8 cups spinach

chilli flakes/hot red pepper flakes (optional)

crudités, to serve

6 ceramic ramekins

SERVES 6

Preheat the oven to 200°C (400°F) Gas 6.

Cut the artichokes into small bite-sized pieces and set aside.

Put the macadamia nuts, non-dairy milk, salt, garlic and nutritional yeast in a high-speed blender and blend until completely smooth.

Sauté the onions in a little olive oil in a large frying pan/skillet set over a medium heat. Once browned, pour in the macadamia nut mixture and stir in the arrowroot. The mixture will start to thicken.

Divide the spinach and artichokes between your ramekins and pour some of the warm macadamia mixture over the vegetables. Sprinkle each ramekin with chilli flakes/hot red pepper flakes, if using.

Place the filled ramekins on a baking sheet and bake in the preheated oven for about 18 minutes, or until the tops have firmed up.

Serve immediately with your choice of crudités. This is best eaten warm.

BLACK BEAN DIP

A GREAT ONE TO SERVE WITH TORTILLA CHIPS OR (BELL) PEPPER STRIPS.

2 teaspoons extra virgin olive oil

1/4 onion, diced

1 tomato, diced

1 x 400-g/14-oz. can of black beans, rinsed

2 teaspoons of freshly chopped coriander/cilantro

1 teaspoon ground cumin

pinch of sea salt

pinch of freshly ground black pepper

1/2 teaspoon chilli/chili powder (optional)

freshly squeezed juice of 1 lime

2 spring onions/scallions, chopped

Heat 1 teaspoon of the olive oil in a saucepan over a medium heat. Fry the onion and tomato until soft and the onions have browned, then allow to cool for a few minutes.

Transfer the onion and tomato to a food processor and add the black beans, coriander/cilantro, cumin, salt, pepper and chilli/chili powder, if using. Pulse until mostly smooth, to your preference – you may want it a little on the chunky side. Garnish with the remaining olive oil and the spring onions/scallions.

GARLIC & WHITE BEAN DIP

SPREAD THIS DIP ONTO THICK, CRUSTY BREAD OR SERVE WITH CRUDITÉS.

2 garlic cloves, skin on

1 x 400-g/14-oz. can of butter beans

1 tablespoon freshly squeezed
  lemon juice

1/2 teaspoon sea salt

1 teaspoon dried oregano

1/2 teaspoon dried rosemary

4 tablespoons extra virgin olive oil

Preheat the grill/broiler to medium.

Put the garlic cloves on a baking sheet and grill/broil for 2–3 minutes until they have roasted. Watch them closely as they burn easily.

Remove the skins from the garlic cloves and put the garlic in a food processor with the butter beans, lemon juice, salt, oregano, rosemary and 3 tablespoons of the olive oil. Blitz until smooth, then pour the remaining olive oil on top.

SERVES 2

ZESTY ALMOND PESTO

TRADITIONALLY, PESTO IS MADE WITH BASIL, PINE NUTS AND PARMESAN. THIS CHEESE-FREE VERSION IS MADE WITH A MIXTURE OF HERBS AND ALMONDS IN PLACE OF THE PINE NUTS. THE ZINGY FLAVOURS FROM THE KAFFIR LIME LEAF AND THE LEMON ZEST MAKE IT TASTE MORE ASIAN THAN ITALIAN.

20 g/1 cup each spinach, fresh mint, parsley and coriander/cilantro, tightly packed

30 g/¼ cup blanched almonds

6 tablespoons extra virgin olive oil, plus extra to preserve

1 kaffir lime leaf (or substitute lemongrass)

freshly squeezed juice of 1 lime

grated zest of 1 lemon

1 garlic clove

pinch of sea salt

Put all the ingredients in a food processor and blitz until they turn into a paste. Store in an airtight container in the fridge for up to 4 days. Pour more olive oil onto the pesto to preserve its bright green colour, if you like.

LIGHTER GUACAMOLE

GUAC IS ONE OF THOSE FOODS THAT'S SO EASY TO DIG INTO AND FINISH A WHOLE BOWL OF WITHOUT EVEN TRYING. THIS VERSION INCLUDES A HEFTY DOSE OF FRESH PEAS AND EXTRA VEGGIES, WHICH ALLOW THE DIP TO KEEP ITS CREAMY TEXTURE AND BODY, BUT WHICH MELLOW OUT THE DENSITY OF THE AVOCADO.

1 large avocado, pitted

90 g/1½ cups peas, ideally fresh, but frozen and thawed is fine too

½ red (bell) pepper, deseeded

2 tomatoes

¼ small onion

1 garlic clove

large handful of fresh coriander/cilantro

freshly squeezed juice of ½ lime

1 tablespoon freshly squeezed lemon juice, plus extra to preserve

Put all the ingredients in a food processor and blitz until smooth. Serve immediately; or if keeping in the fridge, squeeze more lemon juice onto the surface of the dip to prevent the avocado from browning.

SERVES 2-3

GRISSINI WITH CARAWAY SEEDS

GRISSINI ARE A GREAT SNACK AND A VERY POPULAR PARTY FOOD.
THEY'RE ACTUALLY EASY TO MAKE AND CAN BE SERVED ALONGSIDE
VIRTUALLY ANY DIP OR JUST MUNCHED ON THEIR OWN.

140 ml/$\frac{2}{3}$ cup lukewarm water

5 g/1 teaspoon active dry yeast

1 teaspoon barley malt or other
sweetener

190 g/1$\frac{1}{2}$ cups strong unbleached
bread flour

30 g/$\frac{1}{4}$ cup strong wholemeal/
whole-wheat bread flour

30 g/$\frac{1}{4}$ cup fine cornmeal

$\frac{1}{2}$ teaspoon salt

$\frac{1}{2}$ teaspoon caraway seeds

3 tablespoons olive oil

baking sheets, lined with
baking parchment

MAKES 20

Whisk the water, yeast and barley malt together in a small
bowl, cover and allow to rest for 15 minutes. The yeast will
start to foam slightly while it is resting.

In a separate bowl, mix the flours, cornmeal, salt, caraway
seeds and 2 tablespoons of the oil. Add the bubbly yeast
mixture and mix until it comes together. Transfer to a lightly
floured surface and knead until smooth – about 4 minutes.
Place on a prepared baking sheet and, using a silicone
spatula, rub oil lightly over the dough. Put in the oven with
only the light on and allow to rise for 1 hour.

After 1 hour, preheat the oven to 180°C (350°F) Gas 4.

Take the dough out of the oven and shape it into a flat
oval. Using a sharp knife, cut the dough into strips 1 cm/
½ inch wide. Pull and stretch each strip into a long stick.
Some strips will be longer and thicker so you'll be able to
stretch 2 or 3 grissini out of them. You should get about
20 grissini roughly 35 cm/14 inches long. They puff up a
little while baking. Don't use a rolling pin to stretch them as
that flattens them too much and pushes out the air.

Place the stretched grissini back on the prepared baking
sheets spaced 7 mm/⅓ inch apart. Brush a little oil over
each one and bake in the preheated oven, in batches, for
12–15 minutes, turning the grissini over halfway through
baking. Allow to cool on the baking sheets and store in a
sealed bag for about 10 days.

RYE & OLIVE-OIL CRACKERS

IT'S EASY TO MAKE CRACKERS — ALL YOU NEED IS 20 MINUTES TO MAKE A BATCH. THEY WILL ALWAYS BE SO MUCH HEALTHIER THAN THE STORE-BOUGHT VERSION AND EXACTLY TO YOUR TASTE.

130 g/³/₄ cup rye flour

130 g/³/₄ cup unbleached plain/all-purpose flour

2 tablespoons unhulled sesame seeds

¹/₂ teaspoon salt, or to taste

freshly ground black pepper, to taste

50 g/¹/₄ cup olive oil

1 teaspoon brown rice syrup

baking sheet, lined with baking parchment

MAKES ABOUT 16

Mix together the flours, seeds, salt and some pepper in a bowl. In a separate bowl, whisk together the oil, 60 ml/¹/₄ cup water and the syrup to emulsify. Slowly pour into the bowl of dry ingredients, stirring until well combined. The dough should quickly form a ball and shouldn't be sticky. Knead a couple of times, just enough to make sure all the ingredients are evenly distributed. Wrap the dough in clingfilm/plastic wrap and allow to rest at room temperature for 10 minutes.

Divide the dough into 3 equal portions.

Preheat the oven to 200°C (400°F) Gas 6.

Place the dough between 2 sheets of baking parchment and roll it out very thinly. If you like really crunchy crackers, the dough should be almost paper-thin, but if you like a bit of texture, roll it to your preferred thickness.

Use a knife or a pizza cutter to cut out squares or rectangles, re-rolling any trimmings. Transfer the crackers to the prepared baking sheet. Prick each one a couple of times with a fork.

Bake in the preheated oven for about 4–7 minutes, depending on the thickness of the crackers. They shouldn't brown, just get slightly golden. They will firm up as they cool, so don't expect them to be crunchy straight out of the oven! Allow to cool completely and store in an airtight container for 1–2 weeks.

HOMEMADE CORN TORTILLA CHIPS

THESE CHIPS ARE MADE WITHOUT ADDING ANY OTHER TYPE OF
FLOUR EXCEPT FOR THE CORNMEAL BECAUSE THE TASTE IS
DELICIOUS AND IT ALSO MEANS THEY ARE GLUTEN-FREE. BUT
THEY MUST BE EATEN SOON AFTER BAKING, OTHERWISE THEY
TURN HARD. SUBSTITUTE HALF THE AMOUNT OF CORNMEAL WITH
WHEAT OR SPELT FLOUR IF YOU WANT THEM TO KEEP FOR LONGER.

130 g/1 cup finely ground yellow cornmeal

½ teaspoon sea salt, or to taste

1 tablespoon sesame seeds

1 tablespoon olive oil

240 ml/1 cup boiling water

MAKES 20–24

Preheat the oven to 150°C (300°F) Gas 2.

In a bowl, combine the cornmeal, salt and sesame seeds.
Whisk, then add the oil and boiling water. Stir until well
incorporated; you should get a soft dough, but not sticky.

Cut two pieces of baking parchment to the size of your
baking sheet. Place one paper on the work surface and
top with the dough, then top the dough with the second
piece of paper. Use a rolling pin to roll out the dough
about 1 mm/¹⁄₁₆ inch thick.

Bake in the preheated oven for 10 minutes. Take out and
mark with a knife into triangle shapes, or shapes of your
choice. Continue baking for another 7–10 minutes, just
until the dough stops being soft. Overbaking will make the
chips too hard, so be careful! Let cool and break into the
marked shapes. Serve the same day while still warm.

BLACK SESAME SEED CRACKERS

THESE HOME-BAKED CRACKER SNACKS ARE SO USEFUL TO HAVE STORED AWAY FOR WHEN HUNGER STRIKES.

260 g/2 cups flour of your choice, or a combination of 2–3 different kinds, if you like, chilled (yes, chilled!)

¼ teaspoon salt

4 teaspoons baking powder

140 g/1 cup non-hydrogenated margarine, chilled

1 tablespoon brown rice syrup

50 ml/¼ cup ice-cold plain soy milk or water, or as needed

TOPPING

black sesame seeds (or other seeds like sesame, caraway or cumin, or dried herbs such as oregano or basil etc.)

coarse sea salt

pastry wheel or cookie cutter

Put the flour, salt and baking powder in a food processor and pulse to mix. Add the margarine and pulse 6–8 times until the mixture resembles coarse breadcrumbs. Add the syrup and pulse again. Gradually add the ice-cold milk or water one tablespoon at a time, pulsing until the mixture just begins to clump together. If you pinch some of the crumbly dough and it holds together, it's ready. If the dough doesn't hold together, add a tiny bit more liquid and pulse again.

Place the dough on a lightly floured work surface. Knead it just enough to form a ball. Shape it into a disc, wrap it in clingfilm/plastic wrap and refrigerate it for at least 1 hour, and up to 2 days. Allow the dough to rest at room temperature for 5–10 minutes before rolling it out.

Preheat the oven to 180°C (350°F) Gas 4.

Place the dough on a sheet of lightly floured baking parchment and roll it out until 1 mm/¹⁄₃₂ inch thick. Use a pastry wheel to cut it into sticks, or stamp out shapes with a cookie cutter. Space the crackers out evenly and slide the baking paper onto a baking sheet.

For the topping, lightly brush each cracker with water and sprinkle the black sesame seeds over the top. Salt lightly.

Bake in the preheated oven for 10 minutes, or until the dough puffs up a little and turns golden. Allow to cool completely on the baking sheet. Store in an airtight container for up to 2 weeks.

PARTY PIECES

MINI BRUSCHETTAS

YOU CAN WHIP UP A PLATTER OF THESE DELICIOUS, FRESH-TASTING BITES WITH THE MINIMUM OF EFFORT.

2 ciabatta, sliced and lightly toasted

OLIVE & CAPER TOPPING

500 g/4 cups pitted black olives

2 garlic cloves, crushed

4 tablespoons capers, well rinsed

grated zest and juice of 2 lemons

1 teaspoon chilli/hot red pepper flakes

pinch of sugar

splash of extra virgin olive oil

handful freshly chopped flat-leaf parsley

TOMATO & PEPPER TOPPING

2 red (bell) peppers, deseeded

400 g/14 oz. fresh plum tomatoes

2 garlic cloves, whole and unpeeled

6 tablespoons olive oil

FRESH HERB PESTO TOPPING

2 large handfuls fresh flat-leaf parsley and 1 large handful fresh basil leaves

2 garlic cloves, crushed

grated zest and juice of 2 lemons

100 g/³⁄₄ cup pine nuts, lightly toasted

6 tablespoons extra virgin olive oil

To make the olive and caper topping, whizz the olives, garlic, capers, lemon zest, chilli/hot red pepper flakes, sugar, olive oil and parsley in a blender. It can either be slightly chunky or puréed, as you prefer. Season to taste with lemon juice, salt (if needed as olives can be very salty), pepper and an extra pinch of sugar if the olives have a particularly sour edge.

For the tomato and pepper topping, preheat the oven to 200°C (400°F) Gas 6.

Halve the (bell) peppers and put them with the tomatoes, and garlic on a baking sheet lined with foil, sprinkle with salt and drizzle with olive oil, and put in the preheated oven. Remove the garlic when it is soft (after 10–15 minutes) and set aside. Remove the tomatoes after 20–25 minutes. Remove the peppers after 30 minutes, when their skins have coloured, and put them in a sealed plastic bag. Once the tomatoes are cool, remove the skins and put the flesh in a bowl. Squeeze the garlic cloves out of their skins into the same bowl. Remove the cooled peppers from the plastic bag and peel away their skins. Roughly chop the peppers and tomatoes and put them back in the bowl. Mix and season to taste with salt and pepper.

For the herb pesto topping, combine all the ingredients in a bowl and add half the lemon juice. Lightly pulse in a small blender and season to taste with salt and pepper.

Serve the assorted toppings on lightly toasted ciabatta slices. Assemble just before you are ready to serve.

MAKES 16 TOPPINGS EACH

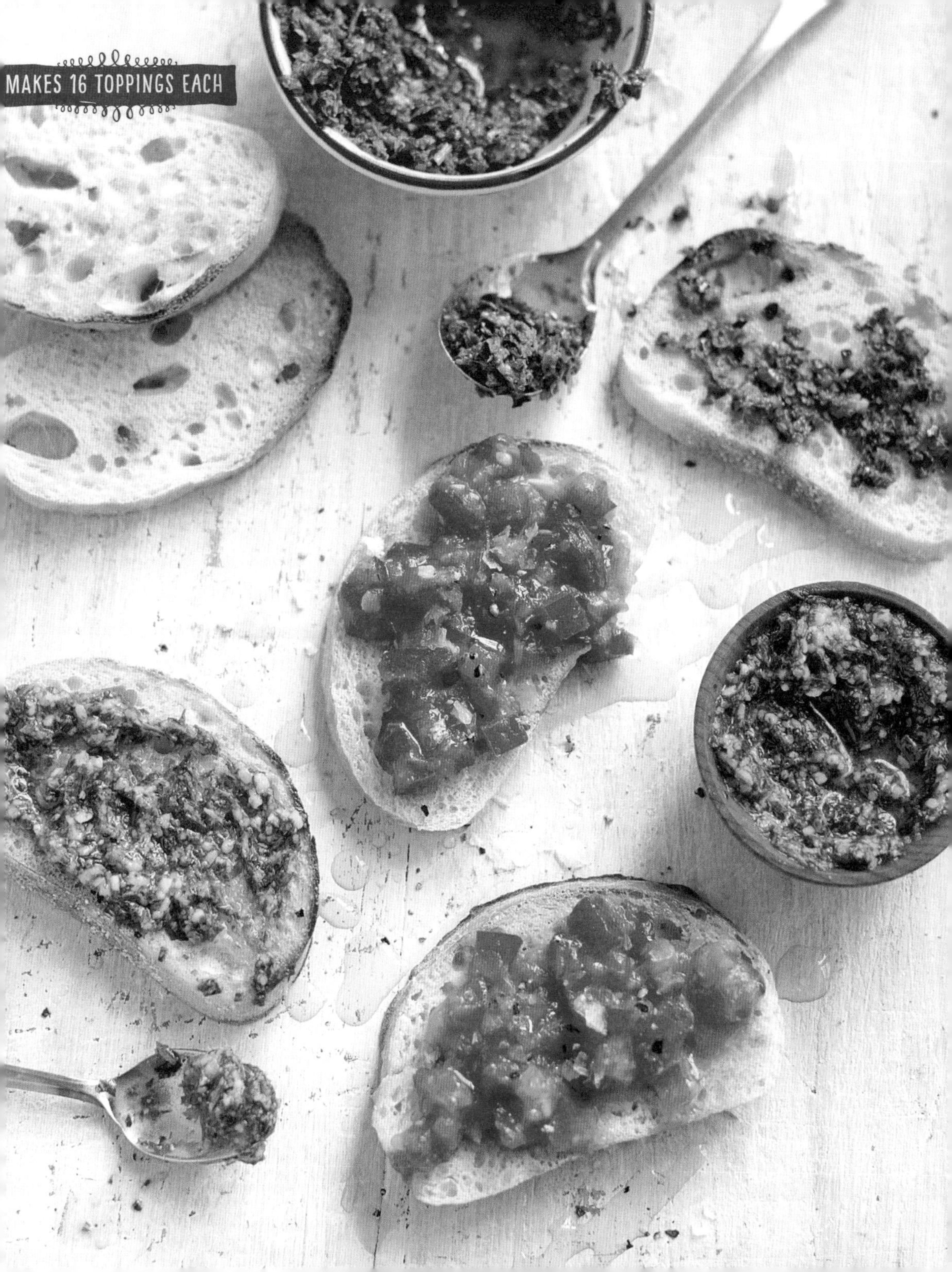

CAPONATA

IN ITALY, CAPONATA IS EATEN WARM AS A SIDE DISH OR COLD AS PART OF AN ANTIPASTO SELECTION. IT IS ALSO DELICIOUS SERVED AT ROOM TEMPERATURE ON TOASTED CIABATTA SLICES, AS HERE.

1 aubergine/eggplant, cubed

1 teaspoon cinnamon

2 tablespoons olive oil

1 red onion, chopped

2 celery stalks, sliced

1 garlic clove, crushed

1 x 400-g/14-oz. can chopped tomatoes

handful of sultanas/golden raisins

2 tablespoons vegan white wine

2 teaspoons capers, drained

1 tablespoon white wine vinegar

2 teaspoons sugar

squeeze of fresh lemon juice

TO SERVE

handful of freshly chopped flat-leaf parsley leaves

drizzle of extra virgin olive oil

freshly squeezed lemon juice

slices of ciabatta, toasted

Season the aubergine/eggplant cubes generously with salt and pepper, and sprinkle with cinnamon. Heat the oil in a large frying pan/skillet set over a low heat, add the aubergine/eggplant and cook for about 10 minutes until soft and turning golden. Remove the aubergine/eggplant from the pan and set aside until needed.

Return the pan to the heat and add the onion, celery and garlic, and cook for about 8 minutes until the vegetables begin to soften. Add the tomatoes, sultanas/golden raisins and wine, and simmer over a low heat for about 20 minutes. Stir in the cooked aubergine/eggplant, add the capers, vinegar, sugar and lemon juice, and cook over a low heat until the taste of vinegar softens. Remove from the heat and allow to cool to room temperature.

Stir in the parsley and add a drizzle of olive oil and a squeeze of lemon juice. Spoon onto slices of toasted ciabatta to serve.

SERVES 4-6

RAW SEED FALAFELS

HERE'S A FRY-FREE AND CHICKPEA-FREE FALAFEL THAT'S
SURPRISINGLY EASY TO MAKE. IT'S ALSO A GREAT LUNCHBOX
ITEM AND THE MIX CAN STAY FRESH IN THE FRIDGE FOR DAYS.
THESE GREEN BALLS GO WITH JUST ABOUT ANYTHING – SERVE AS
A SNACK WITH HUMMUS OR EVEN AS AN APPETIZER WITH SALAD.
IT'S A GREAT WAY TO INTRODUCE MORE SEEDS INTO YOUR DIET!

130 g/1 cup pumpkin seeds

130 g/1 cup sunflower seeds

50 g/$\frac{1}{2}$ cup walnuts

**5 tablespoons freshly chopped flat-leaf
parsley**

5 dried tomato halves, soaked

2 garlic cloves, crushed

3 tablespoons olive oil

freshly squeezed juice of $1\frac{1}{2}$ a lemon

1 teaspoon dried oregano

sea salt and crushed black pepper

Grind the seeds in a food processor or blender into a fine
flour, making sure you don't process them for too long,
otherwise they might turn into seed butter. Finely chop the
walnuts, as they'll give the falafels a nice crunchy texture.
Add them, together with the remaining ingredients, to the
seed flour and mix well with your hands or with a silicone
spatula. Taste and adjust the seasoning if necessary – it
should taste strong and full of flavour. Try squeezing the
seed mixture in your hand and if it doesn't fall apart it's
moist enough. In case it feels dry and crumbles
immediately, add 1 tablespoon of water and mix again.

Form the mixture into walnut-sized falafel balls and either
serve immediately or keep refrigerated before use.

SERVES 24

CHERRY TOMATOES FILLED WITH SPINACH PESTO

THESE SMALL, DELICATE BITES ARE A REAL TREAT, NOT ONLY BECAUSE OF THEIR FRESH TASTE BUT ALSO BECAUSE THE BRIGHT RED AND LIGHT GREEN COMBINATION OF COLOURS REALLY GETS NOTICED! THEY CAN BE SERVED NOT ONLY AS APPETIZERS BUT ALSO AS AMUSE-BOUCHE, TO IMPRESS YOUR GUESTS.

20 cherry tomatoes

2 handfuls of baby spinach

85 g/²⁄₃ cup sunflower seeds

4 tablespoons olive oil

2 garlic cloves, peeled

1 teaspoon lemon juice (to prevent oxidation of greens)

sea salt

MAKES 20

Wash the tomatoes and remove their stems. Next, cut a very thin layer off the bottom of each tomato so that they can sit on a serving plate without rolling. Slice off the tops and scoop out the flesh with a small spoon to make enough space for the filling. Do this carefully so as not to damage the tomatoes.

Wash and drain the spinach well. Lightly dry-roast the sunflower seeds to release their full aroma. Place all the ingredients (except the tomatoes) in a blender and blend until smooth. Add 1 tablespoon of water if necessary; the pesto should be liquid enough to be easily spooned or piped into the cored cherry tomatoes.

Fill each tomato carefully and serve immediately on fresh lettuce and seed sprouts, if desired.

Tip: If in season, use wild garlic/ramps instead of spinach for a beautiful aroma and an even more fluorescent green colour! Other soft greens and herbs work well, too. Also, you can use almonds, pine nuts, hazelnuts, sesame seeds, cashews and any other nuts and seeds instead of sunflower seeds to make this pesto.

LETTUCE WRAPS WITH CHILLI SAUCE

BABY GEM HEARTS HAPPEN TO BE THE PERFECT SHAPE TO BE USED AS WRAPS AND HOLD A FILLING. THESE MAKE LOVELY LIGHT SNACKS TO SERVE AT AN INFORMAL DINNER PARTY.

2 heads of Baby Gem lettuce

handful of fresh coriander/cilantro

2–3 spring onions/scallions

2 large carrots

1 pomegranate

SWEET CHILLI SAUCE

1–2 fresh chillies/chiles, to taste

1 garlic clove, crushed

½ teaspoon onion powder

125 ml/½ cup rice vinegar

2 big teaspoons stevia

½ teaspoon sea salt

1 tablespoon cornflour/cornstarch

spice grinder (optional)

MAKES 10–12

Tear 10–12 larger leaves off the Baby Gem lettuce – these will become your 'wraps'. Wash and arrange on a plate.

To assemble the filling, shred the remaining lettuce as finely as you can. Do the same with the coriander/cilantro and spring onions/scallions, and place all three in a large bowl. Peel the carrots into ribbons and add to the bowl.

For the pomegranate, cut the fruit in half and place in a bowl of cold water. Then tear the flesh and separate the seeds by hand. The seeds will sink to the bottom of the bowl, and the white flesh will float. Pour away the water and flesh so that you are left with the seeds. Add the seeds to the vegetables and mix well. Use a spoon to fill the lettuce wraps with the mixture.

For the sweet chilli sauce, using a spice grinder, grind the chillies to a paste. If you don't have one of these, slice the chillies/chiles as thinly as possible. Put the chillies, garlic, onion powder, rice vinegar, 125 ml/½ cup water, the stevia and salt in a saucepan over medium heat and bring to the boil. Simmer for about 8–10 minutes until reduced.

Meanwhile, put the cornflour/cornstarch in a small bowl with 2 tablespoons water and stir until combined. Turn the heat down to low and slowly stir in the cornflour/cornstarch mixture until the sauce has thickened.

To serve, eat the lettuce wraps by hand, dipping them into the sweet chilli sauce as you go!

COURGETTE UN-FRIES

INSPIRED BY THE MOREISH DEEP-FRIED COURGETTE/ZUCCHINI
SIDE DISH SERVED IN SOME RESTAURANTS, THIS BRILLIANT SNACK
VERSION IS BAKED INSTEAD OF FRIED.

80 ml/⅓ cup almond milk

35 g/¼ cup quinoa flour

35 g/¼ cup ground flaxseeds/linseeds

1 teaspoon garlic powder

½ teaspoon onion powder

½ teaspoon freshly ground black pepper

½ teaspoon sea salt

2 large courgettes/zucchini, cut into
5-mm/¼-inch slices

baking sheet lined with baking parchment

SERVES 3–4

Preheat the oven to 220°C (425°F) Gas 7.

Put the almond milk in a bowl and set aside. Put all the remaining ingredients (except the courgettes/zucchini) in a separate, wide bowl and mix well.

Place each slice of courgette/zucchini into the almond milk, one at a time, then dip into the dry mixture. Once fully coated, place on the prepared baking sheet.

Bake the fries in the preheated oven for 15 minutes. Remove from the oven, flip the slices over, and bake for another 15 minutes. Keep a close eye on them, as they burn easily.

They can be served warm from the oven or at room temperature. Store in an airtight container for up to 3 days.

CREOLE CAULIFLOWER

CREOLE RUB IS A MIX OF SOUTHERN AMERICAN FLAVOURS
NORMALLY USED TO FLAVOUR MEAT; IT GIVES A FANTASTIC ZING
TO THESE CAULIFLOWER BITES. YOU DO HAVE TO MAKE THESE
NIBBLES AHEAD OF TIME, AS THEY TAKE ABOUT 6 HOURS IN THE
OVEN TO BECOME PROPERLY DRY AND CRISP.

1 large head of cauliflower, cut into florets
about 1 cm/½ inch thick

2 tablespoons black treacle/molasses
or maple syrup

4–5 tablespoons tomato passata/strained
tomatoes (or 1 tablespoon tomato paste
mixed with 4 tablespoons water if you
don't have passata on hand)

1 teaspoon cayenne pepper

2 teaspoons paprika

1 teaspoon ground cumin

½ teaspoon dried thyme

½ teaspoon garlic powder

1 teaspoon sea salt

freshly ground black pepper

*baking sheet, lined with
baking parchment*

Preheat the oven to 115°C (225°F) Gas ¼, with the fan on, if
possible.

Wash the cauliflower florets thoroughly, then place in a
large bowl. Put all the remaining ingredients in a separate,
wide bowl and mix well.

Pour the mixture over the cauliflower in the bowl and toss
until well coated.

Scatter the cauliflower on a baking sheet and bake in the
preheated oven for about 6 hours, until thoroughly dried
and crisp.

SERVES 6

COURGETTE & WALNUT CANAPÉS

FRESH, CRUNCHY BUT ALSO QUITE FILLING, THESE LITTLE
CANAPÉS WON'T PASS UNNOTICED! SOME PEOPLE DON'T REALISE
HOW DELICIOUS RAW COURGETTE/ZUCCHINI CAN BE, SINCE IT'S
TRADITIONALLY ALWAYS COOKED (AND MORE OFTEN OVERCOOKED!).
YOU'LL CERTAINLY ENJOY MAKING THESE CANAPÉS AND OFFERING
THEM ROUND TO YOUR FRIENDS AND FAMILY.

140 g/1 cup chopped walnuts

2 tablespoons chopped flat-leaf parsley

**4 dried tomato halves, soaked, drained
and chopped**

½ teaspoon sweet paprika

⅛ teaspoon chilli powder

juice of ½ lemon

a little almond milk or water

**1 medium courgette/zucchini, sliced
diagonally into 3-mm/⅛-inch slices**

**30 g/½ cup alfalfa, chia and radish or
other seed sprouts**

sea salt

MAKES 20 CANAPÉS

Blend all the ingredients (except the liquid, initially,
courgette/zucchini and the seed sprouts) in a food
processor or blender into a thick paste, seasoning with salt
to taste. You're looking for a dense consistency that will
spread and safely stay on a courgette/zucchini slice, but
add a little almond milk or water if it's too thick. Taste and
add more seasoning, if needed.

Gently pat the courgette/zucchini slices with paper towels
if they're moist. Top with 1–2 teaspoons of the spread and
garnish with some seed sprouts. Continue until you use up
all the courgette/zucchini slices. Serve immediately, since
the saltiness of the spread might make the courgette/
zucchini wilt and let out its moisture. Depending on how
much spread you used for each canapé you might have
some leftover. This spread will keep in the fridge for
a couple of days, so don't worry.

JALAPEÑO ONION RINGS

ONION RINGS FOR SOME EVOKE NOSTALGIC MEMORIES OF CHILDHOOD MEALS. BEFORE WE EVEN TASTE SOMETHING, THE ANTICIPATION OF IT INFLUENCES OUR EVENTUAL ENJOYMENT OF THE FOOD, WHICH IS PERHAPS WHY THIS GROWN UP HEALTHIER VERSION OF THE FRIED SNACK IS A REAL CROWD PLEASER.

3 tablespoons ground flaxseeds/linseeds

170 g/1 cup cornmeal

150 g/1 cup gluten-free crackers, processed into crumbs

1 large fresh jalapeño pepper, thinly sliced and deseeded if you don't like things too spicy

½ teaspoon sea salt

freshly ground black pepper

2 large onions, cut into 2-cm/1-inch thick slices

2 baking sheets, lined with foil

MAKES ABOUT 36

Preheat the oven to 220°C (425°F) Gas 7.

Mix the flaxseeds/linseeds with 175 ml/⅔ cup water and set aside. Separately, mix the cornmeal, cracker crumbs, jalapeño, salt, and pepper to taste in a wide bowl.

Separate the onion slices into rings. Dip them into the flaxseed/linseed mixture, then into the crumb mixture. For each onion ring, do this twice so that they are double-coated.

Arrange the rings on the prepared baking sheets and bake in the preheated oven for 8–12 minutes until they are slightly browned on the outside and cooked all the way through.

AUBERGINE & SUMAC FRIES

THE VELVETY SMOOTH TEXTURE OF AUBERGINE/EGGPLANT IS THE
PERFECT VEHICLE FOR SOME WONDERFUL MIDDLE EASTERN
INGREDIENTS: SESAME SEEDS, MINT, SUMAC AND LEMON. ZINGY,
ZESTY AND FRESH, THESE 'FRIES' ARE A REAL TREAT.

500 g/1 lb. 2 oz. aubergine/eggplant,
ends trimmed and cut into 2-cm/³⁄₄-inch
wide strips

125 g/1 cup rice flour

1 tablespoon sumac, plus extra
to serve

2–3 sprigs fresh mint, leaves stripped and
very finely chopped

1 teaspoon fine salt

vegetable oil

1 tablespoon toasted sesame seeds

lemon wedges and tahini yogurt dip, to
serve (optional)

**SERVES 2-4
AS A SIDE**

A few hours before serving (ideally 2–12 hours), put the
aubergine/eggplant in a large bowl and add cold water
and some ice to cover. Set a plate on top to weigh
the aubergine/eggplant down; it must stay submerged.

When ready to cook, combine the rice flour, sumac,
chopped mint and salt in a shallow bowl and mix well.

Fill a large saucepan one-third full with the oil or, if using
a deep-fat fryer, follow the manufacturer's instructions. Heat
the oil to 190°C (375°F) or until a cube of bread browns
in 30 seconds.

Working in batches, transfer the damp aubergine/eggplant
to the rice flour mixture and coat lightly. Place in a frying
basket and lower into the hot oil carefully. Fry until golden,
3–4 minutes. Remove and drain on paper towels. Repeat
until all of the aubergine/eggplant has been fried.

Mound on a platter and scatter over the sesame seeds,
some sumac and the mint leaves. Serve with lemon wedges
and a tahini yogurt dip, if you like.

GARLIC & HERB POTATO WEDGES WITH GARLIC LEMON MAYO

THE SMELL OF ROASTING GARLIC AND ROSEMARY INFUSES THESE POTATO WEDGES WITH SUNNY MEDITERRANEAN FLAVOURS. TO KEEP THE GOOD FEELINGS GOING, SERVE WITH THE VEGAN GARLIC MAYO DIP AND IT WILL SEEM LIKE SUMMER, NO MATTER WHAT THE WEATHER.

800 g/1¾ lbs. floury potatoes, preferably Cyprus, scrubbed

4–5 tablespoons vegetable oil

1 teaspoon fine salt

2 garlic cloves, crushed

1 teaspoon dried rosemary

1 teaspoon dried thyme

salt and freshly ground black pepper

GARLIC LEMON MAYO

125 g/1 cup plus 1 tablespoon vegan mayonnaise

2 garlic cloves, crushed

freshly squeezed juice of ½ lemon

2 x baking sheets, lined with baking parchment

Preheat the oven to 200°C (400°F) Gas 6.

In a small bowl, combine the mayonnaise, garlic and lemon juice and stir to mix. Set aside.

Cut the potatoes in half lengthwise, then into thirds so you end up with six long wedges per potato. Put the wedges in a large mixing bowl and add the oil, salt, garlic, herbs and a generous grinding of pepper. Toss well with your hands to coat evenly, then transfer to the prepared baking sheets and spread evenly in a single layer.

Roast for 20 minutes in the preheated oven, then turn the potatoes and continue roasting for another 10–15 minutes, until golden and cooked through. Sprinkle with salt and more pepper and serve with the garlic lemon mayo.

SERVES 4-6

BUTTERNUT FRIES

THESE FRIES HAVE A 'CHILLI CHEESE' FLAVOUR COATING, PERFECT FOR CURING THOSE CHEESY CRAVINGS!

1 medium butternut squash, peeled

1 small red chilli/chile

4 tablespoons cashew butter

1 tablespoon olive oil

1 teaspoon salt

2 tablespoons nutritional yeast

sweet and spicy sauce (try Frank's hot sauce), to serve

baking sheet, greased and lined with baking parchment

Preheat the oven to 220°C (425°F) Gas 7.

Slice the butternut squash into batons and set aside. Thinly slice the red chilli/chile into small pieces, discarding the seeds and mix together with the cashew butter, oil and salt in a bowl.

Add the fries to the mixture and toss to coat, then dip each one in the nutritional yeast. Transfer to the prepared baking sheet and bake in the preheated oven for 40 minutes, turning halfway through cooking. Remove from the oven and serve with sweet and spicy sauce.

BAKED JICAMA FRIES

THIS WONDERFUL VEGETABLE MAKES A GREAT LOW-CARB VERSION OF CLASSIC FRENCH-FRIES.

1 jicama/water chestnut

1½ teaspoons paprika

½ teaspoon garlic powder

1 teaspoon onion powder

¾ teaspoon salt

baking sheet, greased and lined with baking parchment

Preheat the oven to 180°C (350°F) Gas 4.

Peel the jicama and slice it into thin matchsticks. The jicama will be quite moist, so pat the sticks dry between paper towels.

Once dry, put the jicama sticks in a large mixing bowl, add the seasonings and toss to coat.

Transfer the fries to the prepared baking sheet and bake in the preheated oven for 1 hour 10 minutes. Remove from the oven and serve.

SERVES 2

AUBERGINE & COURGETTE ROLL-UPS

THESE TASTY, HERB-RICH ROLL-UPS ARE ONE OF THE BEST WAYS TO SATISFY A HANKERING FOR ITALIAN FOOD, USING DELICIOUS AUBERGINE/EGGPLANT AND COURGETTE/ZUCCHINI.

2 large courgettes/zucchini

1 large aubergine/eggplant

4 teaspoons extra virgin olive oil

1 teaspoon dried thyme

75 g/¾ cup pine nuts

2 tablespoons nutritional yeast

1 tablespoon tomato paste

5–6 sun-dried tomatoes

1 tablespoon dried rosemary

1 teaspoon dried marjoram

½ teaspoon sea salt

freshly ground black pepper

handful of fresh basil leaves

3–4 tablespoons shelled hemp seeds

baking sheet lined with foil

cocktail sticks/toothpicks (optional)

MAKES 12–14

Preheat the grill/broiler to medium.

Cut the courgettes/zucchini and aubergine/eggplant lengthways into long strips about 1 cm/½ inch thick. Arrange them on the prepared baking sheets and lightly brush the aubergine/eggplant with 1 teaspoon of the olive oil. Scatter the thyme over the vegetables. Grill/broil for about 3 minutes, then flip them over and grill/broil for another 3 minutes. Watch them carefully so that they don't burn. You may have to remove the courgettes/zucchini at this point and leave the aubergine/eggplant in for another 1–2 minutes. Once done, set them aside to cool.

Put the remaining olive oil, pine nuts, nutritional yeast, tomato paste, sun-dried tomatoes, rosemary, marjoram and salt in a food processor with 80 ml/⅓ cup water and blitz until very smooth.

Take one vegetable strip, gently spread a thin layer of the mixture over it, lay some basil leaves on top and sprinkle with hemp seeds. Roll up the strip and spear with a cocktail stick/toothpick, if necessary, to seal it closed.

JUICY BROWN RICE PATTIES

A VERY BASIC RECIPE MADE OF WHOLEGRAINS AND VEGGIES
THAT CAN BE SERVED EVEN TO SMALL CHILDREN AS A TASTY
SNACK – JUST REMEMBER TO REDUCE THE AMOUNT OF SPICES.

420 g/3 cups cooked short-grain brown rice (cooked 2:1 water to rice ratio)

70 g/$\frac{1}{2}$ cup very finely grated carrot (about 1 carrot)

40 g/$\frac{1}{2}$ cup very finely grated celeriac/celery root

80 g/$\frac{1}{2}$ cup very finely grated onion (1 small onion)

4 garlic cloves, crushed

40 g/$\frac{1}{4}$ cup finely grated smoked tofu (optional)

2 tablespoons freshly chopped parsley or spring onion/scallion greens

salt, pepper, oregano, chilli/chili powder and sweet paprika, to taste

olive oil, for greasing and brushing

dipping sauces, to serve

baking sheet, lined with baking parchment

MAKES ABOUT 24 PATTIES

For this dish the rice has to be carefully cooked; it should be neither soggy nor hard. For best results use freshly cooked rice, but if using leftover rice from the fridge, bring to room temperature first.

Put the cooked rice, grated veggies, garlic, tofu, parsley and some salt, pepper, oregano, chilli/chili powder and paprika in a bowl. Use your hands to knead until the ingredients are well combined. Taste and add more salt, pepper, oregano, chilli/chili powder or paprika if needed.

Wet your hands and try to shape a small burger from the mixture – if it is a little sticky and soft, but the burger keeps its shape, it should be ready. Leave the mixture to sit in the fridge for 1 hour, or longer.

Preheat the oven to 180°C (350°F) Gas 4.

Wet your hands and shape about 24 small patties. Grease the baking parchment with oil and oil each patty with the help of a silicone brush when you place them on the baking sheet.

Bake in the preheated oven for 12–16 minutes or until golden and compact, with a thin, crunchy crust and a juicy inside. Depending on the oven, you might want to turn them halfway through baking. Serve with dipping sauces of your choosing.

CAULI-POPS

THESE CUTE LITTLE POPS ARE PERFECT FOR PRE-DINNER
MUNCHIES. IT'S SO EASY TO OVER-DO IT FILLING UP ON BREADY
CREATIONS, THEN FEEL TOO STUFFED FOR THE MAIN EVENT.
THESE CAULI-POPS ARE JUST ENOUGH TO TAKE THE EDGE OFF,
WITHOUT BEING TOO HEAVY.

1 large head cauliflower, roughly chopped

100 g/½ cup nutritional yeast

3 heaped tablespoons almond flour

1 garlic clove

½ tablespoon onion powder

½ tablespoon dried thyme

freshly ground black pepper

vegetable oil, for frying

za'atar, to coat

baking sheet, greased

cocktail sticks/toothpicks (optional)

SERVES 8

Boil the cauliflower until soft in a pan of water set over medium heat. Once cooked, drain using a colander and pat dry with paper towels.

Put the cooked cauliflower in a food processor and add the remaining ingredients. Pulse until smooth.

Roll large teaspoonfuls of the cauliflower mixture into balls and place on the prepared baking sheet.

Fill a large frying pan/skillet with vegetable oil so it is 2½ cm/1 inch deep. Set over a medium–high heat and, when hot, drop a small amount of the cauliflower batter into the pan – if it sizzles, the oil is ready to cook with. Carefully put the cauliflower balls into the pan and cook for 2–3 minutes on each side.

Remove the cauli-pops with a slotted spoon and drain on paper towels.

Once cooked, spear the cauli-pops with cocktail sticks/toothpicks and roll in za'atar spice mix if desired, then serve immediately. Any leftover cauli-pops can be stored in an airtight container and eaten the next day.

SWEET TREATS

GOOEY CHOCOLATE COOKIES

FULL OF COCOA FLAVOUR AND NOT OVERLY SWEET, THESE COOKIES WILL SATISFY YOUR CHOCOLATE CRAVING INSTANTLY! COOK FOR A LITTLE LONGER IF YOU PREFER THEM CRISP RATHER THAN SOFT.

60 g/2¼ oz. dark/bittersweet vegan chocolate, broken into pieces

65 g/⅓ cup sunflower oil

75 ml/⅓ cup soya/soy milk

200 g/¾ cup rice, maple or agave syrup

¼ teaspoon bourbon vanilla powder

130 g/1 cup unbleached plain/all-purpose flour

2 tablespoons cocoa powder

¼ teaspoon ground cinnamon

¾ teaspoon baking powder

¼ teaspoon sea salt

baking sheet, lined with baking parchment

MAKES ABOUT 24

Melt the chocolate in a heatproof bowl set over a pan of barely simmering water. Do not let the base of the bowl touch the water. In a mixing bowl, whisk the oil, milk, syrup and vanilla. Add the melted chocolate.

Preheat the oven to 180°C (350°F) Gas 4.

Place a sieve/strainer over the bowl containing the liquid ingredients (this way you won't need to use two bowls).

Put the flour, cocoa, cinnamon, baking powder and salt directly in the sieve/strainer and sift everything until it passes through the sieve/strainer net. Use a spatula to incorporate all the ingredients into a smooth batter. It should not slide down the spoon – if it does, chill the batter in the fridge for 10 minutes.

Using a tablespoon, drop the batter onto the prepared baking sheet, 1 cm/⅓ inches apart. Bake for 12–14 minutes. The dough is dark to start with, so it's easy to burn them, and you want them still soft to the touch when you remove them from the oven. So check for doneness after 12 minutes, and bake them for no longer than 14 minutes.

Remove from the oven, slip the baking sheet with cookies onto the kitchen counter or a cold tray and let cool. Store in a cookie jar for a week or so.

PEANUT BUTTER QUINOA COOKIES

THESE PEANUT BUTTER-PACKED COOKIES TASTE REALLY GOOD. HEALTHFUL QUINOA IS USED IN ITS FLAKE AND FLOUR FORM HERE TOO, MAKING THESE TREATS DOUBLY VIRTUOUS.

420 g/1¾ cup smooth peanut butter

75 g/¾ cup xylitol or other sugar substitute

140 ml/¾ cup agave syrup

2 tablespoons of ground flaxseed mixed with 6 tablespoons of water

1 teaspoon vanilla extract

45 g/½ cup quinoa flakes

2 tablespoons quinoa flour

½ teaspoon bicarbonate of soda/ baking soda

baking sheet lined with baking parchment

MAKES 24

Preheat the oven to 180°C (350°F) Gas 4.

Mix all ingredients together in a large mixing bowl.
Once the ingredients are all combined, bring the mixture together in your hands then roll into 21½-cm/1-inch balls and place onto the prepared baking sheet. Using your thumb, press down each ball so it is slightly flattened out.

You can use your fingers for this which is great for getting children involved too.

Bake in the preheated oven for approximately 12 minutes, until the cookies are golden, and serve warm. Store the cookies in an airtight container for up to 3 days.

COFFEE TOFFEE COOKIES

THE FROSTING ADDS SWEETNESS TO THESE DIVINE LITTLE COOKIES, PERFECT FOR COFFEE LOVERS.

30 g/⅓ cup raw cocoa beans (or nibs)

100 g/½ cup coconut oil, softened

100 g/½ cup Demerara sugar

60 ml/¼ cup plain soy milk

2 teaspoons coffee extract

¼ teaspoon apple cider vinegar

200 g/1½ cups unbleached spelt flour

½ teaspoon baking powder

1 tablespoon ground flaxseeds

¼ teaspoon bourbon vanilla powder

2 tablespoons ground almonds

¼ teaspoon salt

¼ teaspoon ground cinnamon

chopped nuts, for sprinkling

FROSTING

65 g/⅓ cup Demerara sugar

1 tablespoon cornflour/cornstarch

2 tablespoons plain soy milk

1 teaspoon coffee extract

baking sheet, lined with baking parchment

MAKES 25

Preheat the oven to 180°C (350°F) Gas 4.

Grind the cocoa beans or nibs in a coffee or spice grinder to a fine powder.

Whisk together the coconut oil, sugar, milk, coffee extract and vinegar. In a separate bowl, sift together the flour and baking powder, then stir in the flaxseeds, vanilla powder, ground almonds, salt, cinnamon and ground cocoa beans or nibs. Tip into the bowl of wet ingredients and mix into a smooth dough.

Divide the dough into 25 and roll into balls. Arrange them on the prepared baking sheets about 2 cm/¾ inch apart. Gently flatten each ball with the back of a spoon. Bake in the preheated oven for 9–10 minutes – they should still be a little soft. Allow to cool on the baking sheets.

For the frosting, to finely grind the sugar in a coffee or spice grinder. Mix the cornflour/cornstarch into the milk in a heatproof bowl. Add the coffee extract and sugar and mix. Set over a saucepan of simmering water (do not let the base of the bowl touch the water) and whisk well for a couple of minutes to allow the starch to thicken slightly. Remove from the heat, then allow to cool for 10 minutes.

Spoon some frosting over each cold cookie and sprinkle chopped nuts over the top. Allow to set for at least 1 hour.

Store in an airtight container at room temperature, or, in the summer months, in the fridge. They will keep for up to 2 weeks.

SPICY OAT COOKIES WITH CASHEWS

THE MIX OF SPICES MAKES THESE MORE OF A WINTER CHOICE,
BUT FEEL FREE TO USE OTHER SPICES, OR OMIT THEM – IT WON'T
CHANGE THEIR CRUNCHINESS OR YUMMINESS AT ALL!

100 g/1 cup rolled oats

160 g/1 cup cashews

**130 g/1 cup unbleached plain/
all-purpose flour**

1/4 teaspoon baking powder

1/2 teaspoon ground cinnamon

1/4 teaspoon ground nutmeg

1/4 teaspoon ground ginger

pinch of chilli powder (optional)

1/4 teaspoon salt

130 g/1/2 cup pure maple syrup

100 g/1/2 cup coconut or sunflower oil

1 tablespoon ground flaxseeds

*baking sheets, lined with baking
parchment*

MAKES ABOUT 30

Preheat the oven to 180°C (350°F) Gas 4.

Coarsely grind the oats in a food processor or spice mill.
Finely grind the cashews in the same way.

Sift the flour, baking powder, cinnamon, nutmeg, ginger,
chilli powder and salt in a bowl, then stir in the ground oats
and cashews. Mix well.

Put the syrup, oil and flaxseeds in a separate bowl and
whisk vigorously. Pour into the bowl of dry ingredients and
mix with a wooden spoon.

Pull off walnut-sized pieces of dough and roll into balls.

Arrange on the baking sheets about 3 cm/1¼ inches apart.
Gently flatten each ball with the help of an oiled spatula or
fish slice.

Bake the cookies in batches in the preheated oven for
10–12 minutes, and take them out as soon as the bottoms
turn slightly golden. Don't worry if they seem soft – they
will harden as they cool down.

Remove from the oven, transfer to a wire rack and allow to
cool. Store in an airtight container for up to 2 weeks.

COUSCOUS & JAM CRUNCHIES

THIS IS A GREAT COOKIE WITH A CRUNCHY TEXTURE FROM THE COUSCOUS AND A SLIGHTLY SOFT CENTRE FILLED WITH JAM/JELLY. A GREAT WAY TO USE UP LEFTOVER STORE-CUPBOARD ESSENTIALS.

120 g/³⁄₄ cup couscous

160 g/1³⁄₄ cups ground almonds

130 g/1 cup unbleached plain/all-purpose flour

1 tablespoon ground flaxseeds

¹⁄₄ teaspoon bourbon vanilla powder

¹⁄₄ teaspoon salt

130 g/¹⁄₂ cup pure maple syrup

100 g/¹⁄₂ cup sunflower oil

1/2 teaspoon almond extract

24 teaspoons/200 g/²⁄₃ cup plum or other thick, naturally sweetened jam/jelly

baking sheets, lined with baking parchment

MAKES ABOUT 24

Preheat the oven to 180°C (350°F) Gas 4.

Put the couscous, almonds, flour, flaxseeds, vanilla powder and salt in a mixing bowl and mix.

Put the syrup, oil and almond extract in a separate bowl and whisk vigorously. Pour into the bowl of dry ingredients and mix with a wooden spoon.

Pull off walnut-sized pieces of dough and roll into balls. Flatten them between your palms until 1 cm/½ inch thick. Arrange them on the baking sheets spaced just slightly apart – they won't spread during baking.

Now use the bottom of a teaspoon, or even better, a teaspoon-sized measuring spoon to gently press a hole in the middle of each cookie. Make circle motions to widen the hole, but don't press too hard otherwise you might break through the bottom of the cookie. Fill each hole with a full teaspoon of jam/jelly. Bake in the preheated oven for 15–16 minutes. Don't worry if they seem soft – they will harden as they cool down.

Remove from the oven and allow to cool on the baking sheets. Store in an airtight container for up to 2 weeks.

COCONUT COOKIES

THESE LUXURIOUS COOKIES WILL NOT LAST LONG IN ANY
HOUSEHOLD! WHAT IS MORE, THE OVAL SHAPE MAKES THESE
PERFECT FOR DUNKING INTO TEA OR HOT COCOA.

130 g/1 cup unbleached spelt or
unbleached plain/all-purpose flour

¼ teaspoon bicarbonate of/baking soda

¼ teaspoon salt

¼ teaspoon bourbon vanilla powder

160 g/2 cups desiccated coconut

75 g/⅓ cup coconut or soy milk

135 g/⅔ cup Demerara sugar

65 g/⅓ cup coconut or sunflower oil

1 tablespoon ground flaxseeds (optional)

50 g/⅓ cup finely chopped vegan dark/
bittersweet chocolate

baking sheet, lined with baking parchment

MAKES ABOUT 20

Preheat the oven to 180°C (350°F) Gas 4.

Sift together the flour, bicarbonate of/baking soda, salt
and vanilla powder in a bowl, then stir in the coconut.

Put the milk, sugar, oil and flaxseeds (if using) in a separate
bowl and whisk vigorously until well combined. Pour into
the bowl of dry ingredients and mix until you get dough
that is firm but a little sticky and not too dry or crumbly.

Wet your hands and pull off a tablespoon of the dough.
You can either roll it into a ball and flatten it between your
palms to get a flat, round cookie, or, roll the tablespoon of
dough into a sausage and then flatten it into an oval.

Continue with the rest of the dough, arranging each cookie
2 cm/¾ inch apart on the prepared baking sheet. Bake in
the preheated oven for 8–10 minutes, no longer! Take them
out as soon as the bottoms turn slightly golden. Don't
worry if they seem soft – they will harden as they cool.

Remove the cookies from the oven, transfer to a wire rack
and allow to cool completely.

Melt the chocolate in a heatproof bowl set over a saucepan
of barely simmering water. Do not let the base of the bowl
touch the water. Drizzle the melted chocolate over the
cooled cookies and allow to set. Store in an airtight
container for up to 2 weeks.

APRICOT & CHOCOLATE BITES

THESE APRICOT AND CHOCOLATE BITES ARE A GREAT EXAMPLE OF A SWEET TREAT THAT JUST DOESN'T NEED BUTTER OR EVEN SUGAR TO MAKE THEM RIDICULOUSLY DELICIOUS!

100 g/²⁄₃ cup dried apricots, chopped

freshly squeezed juice and grated zest of 1 big orange

¼ teaspoon ground ginger

80 g/1 cup desiccated coconut

150 g/1 cup plus 2 tablespoons unbleached plain/all-purpose flour

¼ teaspoon salt

100 g/½ cup coconut oil, melted

70 g/¼ cup brown rice or other syrup

50 g/⅓ cup finely chopped vegan dark/bittersweet chocolate

¼ teaspoon sunflower oil

baking sheets, lined with baking parchment

MAKES 32–33

Preheat the oven to 160°C (325°F) Gas 3.

Put the apricots, orange juice and zest and ginger in a saucepan over a medium heat. Heat until hot but not boiling. Remove from the heat and transfer to a food processor. Blend to a slightly chunky paste.

Put the coconut in a frying pan/skillet and toast over a low-medium heat for about 8 minutes, stirring occasionally, until pale golden. Remove from the pan and allow to cool.

Mix the flour and salt in a bowl and add the toasted coconut. Add the coconut oil to the apricot paste with the syrup and mix well. Now add this to the dry ingredients in the bowl and mix until well incorporated.

Use a small spoon to scoop portions of dough onto the prepared baking sheets. Shape into 32–35 balls, then flatten slightly with the back of the spoon.

Bake the cookies in the preheated oven for 10–12 minutes, just until lightly golden. Allow to cool for a couple of minutes, then transfer to a wire rack to cool completely.

Melt the chocolate in a heatproof bowl set over a saucepan of barely simmering water. Do not let the base of the bowl touch the water. Add the oil and stir until smooth, then allow to cool slightly. Dip each cookie halfway into the melted chocolate. Allow to cool and set completely before serving. Store in an airtight container for up to 2 weeks.

MARBLED ENERGY MUFFINS

BANANA IS THE SECRET INGREDIENT THAT MAKES THESE
MARBLED MUFFINS WONDERFULLY MOIST. TRY TO USE COCONUT
MILK, AS IT GIVES A GREAT CONSISTENCY TO THE MIXTURE.

1 tablespoon raw cocoa nibs

130 g/1 cup unbleached plain/
all-purpose flour

60 g/½ cup plain wholemeal/whole-wheat
flour

¼ teaspoon bourbon vanilla powder

1 teaspoon baking powder

½ teaspoon bicarbonate of/baking soda

¼ teaspoon salt

100 g/½ cup coconut oil, melted

110 ml/½ cup coconut milk

170 ml/¾ cup plain soy milk

½ teaspoon apple cider vinegar

170 g/⅔ cup pure maple syrup

1 ripe banana

¼ teaspoon pure almond extract
(optional)

grated zest of 1 lemon

1 tablespoon raw cocoa powder

12-hole muffin pan lined with
paper cases

Preheat the oven to 180°C (350°F) Gas 4.

In a coffee or spice grinder, grind the cocoa nibs to
a coarse powder.

Sift together the flours, vanilla powder, baking powder,
bicarbonate of/ baking soda and salt in a bowl and mix well.

Put the coconut oil, milks, vinegar, syrup, banana, almond
extract, if using, and lemon zest in a food processor and
blend until smooth. Combine the dry and liquid
ingredients, and mix gently with a silicone spatula.

Spoon one third of the mixture into a separate bowl and
fold in the ground cocoa nibs and cocoa powder.

Divide the plain cake mixture between 10–12 muffin
cases. Put a spoonful of the cocoa mixture on top of that
and, with the help of a chopstick or skewer, mix a little to
get a marbled pattern. Bake the muffins in the preheated
oven for 18–20 minutes. Remove from the muffin pan
and allow to cool on a wire rack before eating.

MAKES 10–12

SUMMER MUFFINS WITH RASPBERRIES & BLACKBERRIES

THIS IS A SIMPLE RECIPE FOR FRUITY, NUTTY MUFFINS. ADDING TOASTED WHEAT GERM GIVES THEM A NICE GOLDEN COLOUR AS WELL AS PROVIDING EXTRA MINERALS, VITAMINS AND FIBRE.

325 g/2½ cups unbleached plain/all-purpose flour

65 g/½ cup plain wholemeal/whole-wheat flour

1½ teaspoons bicarbonate of/baking soda

1 teaspoon baking powder

¼ teaspoon salt

65 g/1 cup finely ground hazelnuts

25 g/3 tablespoons toasted wheat germ (optional)

420 ml/1¾ cups plain soy milk

200 g/¾ cup brown rice syrup

150 g/¾ cup sunflower oil

freshly squeezed juice of ½ lemon

100 g/1 small apple, peeled, cored and chopped

24 raspberries

24 blackberries

12-hole muffin pan lined with paper cases

MAKES 12

Preheat the oven to 180°C (350°F) Gas 4.

Sift together the flours, bicarbonate of/baking soda, baking powder and salt in a bowl and add the ground hazelnuts and wheat germ, if using. Mix well.

Put the milk, syrup, oil, lemon juice and apple in a food processor and blend until smooth.

Combine the dry and liquid ingredients, and mix gently with a silicone spatula. Do not overmix otherwise the muffins will be tough.

Divide the cake mixture between the muffin cases. Gently press 2 raspberries and 2 blackberries into each muffin so that they are half-dipped in the mixture.

Bake in the preheated oven for 25–30 minutes.

Allow to cool in the muffin pan for a few minutes, then transfer to a wire rack to cool completely.

FRUIT-TOPPED BARS

THESE SWEET CAKE BARS ARE TOPPED WITH SOUR CHERRIES TO PROVIDE A NICE CONTRAST IN FLAVOUR, BUT THEY WOULD ALSO WORK WELL WITH RIPE PEACHES, PLUMS, APPLES OR RASPBERRIES.

260 g/2 cups unbleached spelt flour

65 g/$\frac{1}{2}$ cup plain wholemeal/whole-wheat flour

1 teaspoon bicarbonate of/baking soda

1$\frac{1}{2}$ teaspoons baking powder

$\frac{1}{4}$ teaspoon salt

$\frac{1}{4}$ teaspoon bourbon vanilla powder

$\frac{1}{4}$ teaspoon ground cinnamon

few pinches of ground turmeric

80 g/$\frac{1}{2}$ cup hazelnuts or almonds, chopped

360 ml/1$\frac{1}{2}$ cups plain soy yogurt

170 g/$\frac{2}{3}$ cup pure maple syrup

100 g/$\frac{1}{2}$ cup coconut, safflower or other good-quality oil

freshly squeezed juice and grated zest of 1 lemon

1 teaspoon apple cider vinegar

350 g/2 cups pitted sour cherries or cherry plums

23 x 30-cm/9 x 12-in. baking pan, lined with baking parchment

Preheat the oven to 180°C (350°F) Gas 4.

Sift together the flours, bicarbonate of/baking soda, baking powder, salt, vanilla powder, cinnamon and turmeric. Add the nuts and mix everything together.

In a separate bowl, mix the yogurt, syrup, oil, lemon juice and zest and vinegar. Pour into the bowl of dry ingredients and mix gently with a wooden spoon. Do not overmix.

Spoon the mixture into the prepared baking pan and spread level with a spatula.

Scatter the cherries or plums over the surface of the cake mixture, making sure there is some space between the fruit – you don't want to overload the cake with fruit otherwise it will turn out soggy.

Bake the cake in the preheated oven for about 35 minutes, or until golden brown. Remove from the oven and allow to cool in the pan. Slice into squares and drizzle maple syrup over the top to serve.

GINGER & CASHEW GRANOLA BARS

IF YOU'RE ONE OF THOSE PEOPLE WHO IS ALWAYS WORKING
AROUND A BUSY SCHEDULE, YOU'LL BE THANKFUL FOR THIS
RECIPE! BECAUSE THE GRANOLA IS PRE-MADE, THIS TASTY TRAY
JUST REQUIRES ASSEMBLY AND PATIENCE WHILE THE BARS SET.

200 g/1¾ cups plain granola

60 g/½ cup well-chopped cashews

40 g/¼ cup well-chopped crystallized
ginger

80 g/1 cup crisped rice cereal

50 g/¼ cup almond butter

115 g/⅓ cup brown rice syrup

1 tablespoon vegetable oil

20-cm/8-in square baking pan, greased
and lined with baking parchment

MAKES 12

Mix the granola, cashews, ginger and crisped
rice cereal together in a large mixing bowl. Add the
almond butter, rice syrup and oil and mix well so everything
is well-coated.

Press the sticky batter into the pan and set in the fridge
to set for at least 3 hours.

Remove from the fridge and cut into even bars before
serving.

Variation: Candied citrus peel is a great alternative
to crystallized ginger in this recipe and gives the bars
a tropical burst of tangy citrus flavour.

RAFFAELLO SLICES

THESE SLICES ARE A COCONUT-LOVER'S HEAVEN; THE FROSTING ALONE WILL MAKE YOU WISH FOR ANOTHER PORTION...

130 g/1 cup unbleached plain/
all-purpose flour

2 tablespoons cornflour/cornstarch

1 teaspoon baking powder

pinch of salt

pinch of ground turmeric

55 g/²⁄₃ cup desiccated coconut

100 g/½ cup sunflower oil

180 g/²⁄₃ cup brown rice syrup

2 tablespoons plain soy milk

½ teaspoon vanilla extract

1 teaspoon lemon juice

FROSTING

5 tablespoons cornflour/cornstarch

365 ml/1²⁄₃ cups vanilla-flavoured soy milk

100 g/½ cup raw/unrefined brown sugar

¼ teaspoon bourbon vanilla powder

pinch of ground turmeric

100 g/³⁄₄ cup margarine

55 g/²⁄₃ cup desiccated coconut, toasted

large square baking pan, oiled

Preheat the oven to 160°C (325°F) Gas 3.

Sift together the flour, cornflour/cornstarch and baking powder, then mix in the salt, turmeric and coconut. In a separate bowl, mix the oil, syrup, milk, vanilla extract and lemon juice. Pour into the bowl of dry ingredients and mix gently with a spatula until combined.

Spoon the mixture into the prepared baking pan. Bake in the preheated oven, checking after 10 minutes and every 2 minutes thereafter. Remove from the oven as soon as there is a slight change in colour. Let cool a little, then cover with clingfilm/plastic wrap to keep soft while it cools completely.

For the frosting, mix the cornflour/cornstarch into 120 ml/ ½ cup of the milk, then stir in the 2 tablespoons sugar, the vanilla and turmeric. Heat the remaining milk in a saucepan until boiling, then remove from the heat and slowly add the cornflour/cornstarch mixture, whisking vigorously. Return to a low heat and whisk until bubbling. Remove from the heat and allow to cool. Whisk again until smooth again.

Finely grind the remaining sugar in a food processor. In a bowl, beat the margarine with an electric whisk until soft. Gradually add the powdered sugar and beat until light and fluffy. Gently mix in the vanilla cream to a smooth frosting.

Spread the frosting evenly over the cooled base. Sprinkle the coconut over. Wrap in foil and refrigerate for 2 hours before cutting into slices, to serve.

STICKY MOCHA SQUARES

YOU CAN ALSO USE HALF SEMOLINA/FARINA AND HALF UNBLEACHED FLOUR IN THESE IF YOU LIKE, BUT THE GRAINY TEXTURE IS WHAT MAKES THESE SQUARES SO INTERESTING.

30 g/⅓ cup cocoa powder

2 teaspoons bicarbonate of/baking soda

360 g/2 cups semolina/farina

¼ teaspoon salt

230 ml/1 cup plain soy yogurt

230 ml/1 cup plain soy milk

½ teaspoon apple cider vinegar

100 g/½ cup sunflower oil

195 g/¾ cup pure maple syrup

1 teaspoon coffee extract

GLAZE

170 ml/¾ cup non-dairy milk

100 g/3½ oz. vegan dark/bittersweet chocolate, finely chopped

100 g/½ cup coconut oil, melted

¼ teaspoon bourbon vanilla powder

4 tablespoons brown rice or pure maple syrup

1 teaspoon coffee extract

23 x 30-cm/9 x 12-inch baking pan, oiled

MAKES ABOUT 20

Preheat the oven to 180°C (350°F) Gas 4.

Sift together the cocoa powder and bicarbonate of/baking soda into a mixing bowl, then mix in the semolina/farina and salt.

In a separate bowl, whisk together the yogurt, milk, vinegar, oil, syrup and coffee extract. Pour into the bowl of dry ingredients and mix until combined.

Spoon the cake mixture into the prepared baking pan and spread level with a spatula. Bake in the preheated oven for 25 minutes.

Meanwhile, for the glaze heat the milk in a saucepan until hot but not boiling, then remove from the heat, add the chocolate and allow to melt. Stir until smooth. Add the coconut oil, vanilla powder, syrup and coffee extract to the pan and whisk to get a smooth glaze. Keep warm until the cake has finished baking.

Pour the glaze over the hot cake in the pan and allow to cool completely. Most of the glaze will be absorbed by the cake and this is what makes it so moist. Serve at room temperature on the day of baking if possible (or the next day), cut into slices.

BEAN & CASHEW BROWNIES

AT FIRST, THE IDEA OF USING COOKED BEANS IN A BROWNIE
MIXTURE MIGHT SOUND A LITTLE STRANGE, HOWEVER, BLENDED
BEANS GIVE A WONDERFUL TEXTURE TO THESE BROWNIES.

300 g/2 cups canned unsalted haricot/
navy beans (see method for an alternative)

200 g/1½ cups finely chopped vegan
dark/bittersweet chocolate (70% cocoa)

65 g/⅓ cup sunflower oil

130 g/½ cup brown rice or pure maple
syrup

freshly squeezed juice and grated
zest of 1 lemon

80 g/½ cup whole or 80 g/1 cup finely
ground cashews

85 g/⅔ cup unbleached plain/
all-purpose flour

40 g/⅓ cup plain wholemeal/
whole-wheat flour

1 tablespoon baking powder

¼ teaspoon salt

¼ teaspoon ground cinnamon

2 tablespoons apricot jam/jelly, to serve

23 x 30-cm/9 x 12-inch baking
pan, oiled

If you want to cook the haricot/navy beans from scratch,
soak 140 g/¾ cup dried beans in a lot of water overnight.
Drain, cover with three times the volume of water and cook
for 1 hour (or 40 minutes in a pressure cooker). Drain well.

Preheat the oven to 180°C (350°F) Gas 4.

Melt the chocolate in a heatproof bowl set over a saucepan
of barely simmering water. Do not let the base of the bowl
touch the water. Put the melted chocolate, cooked beans,
oil, syrup, lemon juice and zest in a food processor and
blend until smooth.

If using whole cashews, finely grind them in a food
processor or spice mill. Mix the flours, ground cashews,
baking powder, salt and cinnamon in a mixing bowl. Add
the bean mixture and fold in with a spatula until you get
a smooth, very thick consistency.

Spoon the cake mixture into the prepared baking pan and
spread level with a spatula; if it sticks too much, wet it with
warm water and try again. Bake in the preheated oven for
15–20 minutes. Do not overbake – they are supposed to be
a little gooey! Allow to cool completely in the baking pan.

Cut into squares to serve. They are delicious with a little
homemade apricot jam/jelly which contrasts beautifully
with the rich, heavy chocolate taste of these brownies.

COCOA-ALMOND FREEZER FUDGE POPS

THIS FROZEN, CHOCOLATEY NUT-BUTTER CONCOCTION IS A GREAT WAY TO 'UPGRADE' YOUR CHOCOLATE FIX, AND ESPECIALLY GOOD TO EAT AFTER DINNER ON A WARM SUMMER'S EVENING STRAIGHT FROM THE FREEZER. WHEN YOU POP ONE OF THESE FROZEN TREATS INTO YOUR MOUTH, YOU KNOW YOUR BODY WILL BE SATISFIED WITH A HIT OF PURE COCOA.

70 ml/¼ cup almond butter (drain off the oil before measuring)

2 teaspoons ground flaxseeds/linseeds

1 large teaspoon coconut oil

1 large teaspoon xylitol

1½ tablespoons raw unsweetened cocoa powder, plus extra for dusting

½ teaspoon vanilla extract

1 teaspoon espresso powder (optional)

Put all the ingredients in a food processor and blitz until smooth.

Divide the mixture into 8 and roll each portion into a ball between the palms of your hands. Dust in cocoa powder.

Freeze the fudge pops for at least 30 minutes and consume straight from the freezer. Store in the freezer for up to 4 weeks.

MAKES 8

ALMOND BUTTER CUPS

THIS IS A SPIN ON THE CLASSIC AMERICAN CONFECTIONERY, PEANUT BUTTER CUPS. PEANUT BUTTER AND CHOCOLATE IS A GREAT COMBO, BUT ACTUALLY ALMOND BUTTER WORKS BETTER IN THIS RECIPE. ALMONDS ARE ALSO RICH IN VITAMIN E AND CONTAIN LESS SATURATED FAT THAN PEANUTS.

215 ml/1 cup coconut oil

60 g/¾ cup unsweetened cocoa powder

4 tablespoons agave syrup

1 tablespoon stevia (or 2 more tablespoons agave syrup)

dash of vanilla extract

4–5 tablespoons almond butter

1 teaspoon nutritional yeast

pinch of salt (if using unsalted almond butter)

12-hole muffin pan, or 24-hole mini muffin pan, lined with paper cases

Put the coconut oil in a saucepan over low heat and allow to melt. Stir in the cocoa powder, agave syrup, stevia, if using, and vanilla extract until you have smooth liquid chocolate. Divide one third of the mixture between the muffin cases and put the whole muffin pan in the freezer until the mixture has solidified – about 5 minutes.

Meanwhile, mix the almond butter, nutritional yeast and salt, if needed, in a bowl.

Remove the muffin pan from the freezer and place a generous teaspoon of the almond-yeast mixture in the centre of each base of frozen chocolate, then flatten it slightly with your fingers. Pour the remaining melted chocolate over the almond-yeast mixture. Put the whole muffin pan in the freezer again until the mixture has solidified – about 10 minutes.

Remove the almond butter cups from the freezer just before serving to get them at their most firm and crisp. If you store them in the freezer or fridge, they will keep for 3–4 weeks (unless you devour them before!).

MAKES 12 LARGE CUPS, OR 24 MINI CUPS

INDEX

CREDITS

Amy Ruth Finegold
Aubergine dip with almond chia crackers
Beetroot dip with seeded amaranth crackers
Ginger & cashew granola bars
Peanut butter quinoa cookies
White bean & spinach dip

Anya Ladra
Brownie bars
Salty trail mix
Spicy almonds

Caroline Artiss
Berry & baobab bites
Chocolate & avocado balls

Chloe Coker
Caponata
Mini bruschettas
Sweet potato hummus

Dan May
Marinated olives & padrón peppers

Dunja Gulin
Apricot & chocolate bites
Bean & cashew brownies
Black sesame seed crackers
Carob & cocoa 'fudge' bars
Cherry tomatoes filled with spinach pesto
Coconut cookies
Coffee toffee cookies

Courgette & walnut canapés
Couscous & jam crunchies
Fruit topped bars
Gooey chocolate cookies
Grissini with caraway seeds
Homemade corn tortilla chips
Juicy brown rice patties
Marbled energy muffins
Pure energy bars
Raffaello slices
Raw seed falafels
Rye & olive oil crackers
Spicy oat cookies with cashews
Sticky mocha squares
Summer muffins
Very cherry balls

Hannah Miles
Thai green curry popcorn

Jenna Zoe
Almond butter cups
Aubergine & courgette roll-ups
Baked jicama fries
Black bean dip
Bombay mix
Butternut fries
Cauli-pops
Chilli rellenos
Cocoa almond freezer fudge pops
Coconut & spirulina balls

Courgette un-fries
Creole cauliflower
Garlic & white bean dip
Hand-rolled macaroons
Hot spinach & artichoke dip
Jalapeño onion rings
Lettuce wraps with chilli sauce
Lighter guacamole
Masala popcorn with fresh lemonade
NYC-style glazed nuts
Sesame-crusted green beans
Spicy tomato kale chips
Sports bites
Tahini protein bites
Zesty almond pesto

Jordan Bourke
Avocado miso dip with root vegetable chips & dukkah

Laura Washburn
Aubergine & sumac fries
Garlic & herb potato wedges

Vicky Jones
Chickpea fritters

Ursula Ferrigno
Taralli

Food photography by the following:

Ed Anderson pages 2, 33, 34

Tim Atkins page 105

Jan Baldwin page 19

Peter Cassidy page 29

Tara Fisher pages 7, 20, 55

Mowie Kay page 75

William Lingwood pages 12, 46

Steve Painter pages 97, 9

William Reavell pages 16, 41, 56, 81–86, 93, 111, 144

Kate Whitaker pages 45, 49

Clare Winfield pages 1, 5, 8–11, 15, 23, 26, 30, 37, 38, 42, 50, 52, 59–72, 76, 78, 89, 90, 94, 102, 106, 108, 112–140